Joyce McKinney
and the Case of the
Manacled Mormon
by
Anthony Delano

Revel Barker
Publishing

Published as Joyce McKinney and the Manacled Mormon by Mirror Books 1979.
Published as Joyce McKinney and the Case of the Manacled Mormon by Revel Barker Publishing 2009.

ISBN: 978-0-9558238-8-6

Revel Barker Publishing
66 Florence Road
Brighton BN2 8DJ
England

revelbarker@gmail.com

Anthony Delano enjoyed a lengthy career as a foreign correspondent before turning to academic life and writing a PhD thesis, *The Formation of the British Journalist 1900-2000.*
He is now a visiting professor at the London College of Communication, part of the University of the Arts London, a frequent contributor to *BBC History Magazine* and the author of several books, including *Slip-Up: how the* Daily Express *found Ronnie Biggs and Scotland Yard Lost Him.*

This is an affectionate memoir inspired by the newspapermen and women who helped produce the various versions of a classic 20th century Fleet Street saga. Kent Gavin and Mike Molloy had the starring roles but everyone involved knew in their bones what a good story it was and how to go about getting it.

Tidings of Joy...

One of the weirder moments of 2008 for anyone with recollections of the 1970s was a clip shown on television reporting that a biological laboratory in South Korea had cloned a litter of puppies from the hairs of a long dead but sorely missed American pet, a pitbull called Hamburger, or 'Booger'.

So far, so mildly interesting. Then the camera swung to the dead dog's owner, a frumpy middle-aged woman, slobbering over one of the brood and all across Britain men and women of a certain vintage shot off their sofas, pointed at the screen and yelped: 'That's Joyce McKinney!' For those who did not instantly remember her, a simple phrase was enough to remind them: the Manacled Mormon.

The fascination of the story had to be explained to recent generations. It was the resurrection of a truly emblematic personage of late 1970s Britain who enthralled the nation with her outrageous capers only to disappoint it by fleeing the country to avoid being put on trial for what seemed to be a crime never before heard of: in essence, having sex with a man against his will. Joyce herself referred to it as a rape charge.

Joyce McKinney and the intense public fascination with her antics were entertaining in themselves but for all involved – quite a lot of people in the end – the farcical events gained a particular edge from the undercurrent of feverish competition among popular national newspapers for the exclusive rights to her story. The saga that developed could have been scripted for an old Ealing comedy like *Passport to Pimlico* or *The Lavender Hill Mob.*

Entertainments like those old films were no longer in vogue in the Britain of the late 1970s, although the place certainly needed cheering up. Swinging London had been and gone and there was widespread listlessness and foreboding. Things were to get far worse in the couple of years to come but already there were outbreaks of industrial disruption, particularly in the mines and – disturbingly for those making a killing out of Joyce – the newspaper industry. A few landmarks will help to get the period in focus.

In 1977, when the story began, the Labour government of Jim Callaghan was barely staying above water. The Leader of the Opposition, Margaret Thatcher, would soon replace him. Inflation stood at 8.3 per cent, down from 15 per cent the year before, and interest rates hovered around 7.5 per cent. The average house price was £13,650. Home computers were just coming into the shops, *Saturday Night Fever* was the big movie and *Grease* the top musical. People were listening to the Bee Gees, Wings, the Boomtown Rats and the Sex Pistols and watching *Jim'll Fix It* on television. Bing Crosby, Groucho Marx, Maria Callas and Elvis Presley wouldn't see the year out.

Pulling together the story of Joyce's life – the real story – at the time was enormous fun and the dénouement was explosive. The revelations about her seamy fund-raising activities and the pictures that that made such vivid tabloid displays were probably not as shocking to the readers as we editorial entrepreneurs imagined them to be; Britons were fairly relaxed about sex, even then. The value of the story lay in the startling contrast between the sanctimonious persona Joyce had managed to contrive for herself and the grubby – but highly entertaining – reality.

At the time I was the *Daily Mirror*'s chief correspondent in New York. I had recently published *Slip-Up*, a book about another entertaining newsroom farce, the conspiracy between the *Daily Express* and Scotland Yard to get Ronald Biggs, one of the Great Train Robbers, back from Rio de Janeiro and back into a British prison (Revel Barker Books £9.99). These two factors ensured that I was fingered to write the definitive account of Joy's preposterous doings and, of course, the *Mirror*'s spectacular humbling of the *Daily Express*, for Mirror Books. This subsidiary of the newspaper usually contented itself with publishing comics, children's books and collections of columnists' pieces but it had developed ideas above its station.

Writing the book was a good deal less enjoyable than collecting the material. When I began, everyone concerned assumed it would not be published until Joyce had been either acquitted or convicted at the Old Bailey. There was a tight enough schedule to start with but I had just got a first draft together when she and her co-defendant jumped bail and disappeared, soon to surface in the custody of the *Daily Express*.

These fast-moving events meant that helping get together the devastating series that appeared in the paper took priority; although I do not appear as a figure in the book, I did a good deal of reporting on some of the developments. At the same time I had to re-jig the MS on the hoof to include a lot of unforeseen developments. No one at Mirror Books had the time or ability to do any editing and the patchwork MS went to the printers just as it left my hands: a rough draft, really. Setting out to prepare this edition I read the book through for the first time in many years and was appalled at how sloppily put together it was. Still, it came across as a cheerfully diverting story, particularly in regard to the cut-and-thrust newspaper mischief in the heady spirit of the Fleet Street of those times.

This new edition contains a good deal of fresh material, thanks to the inestimable assistance of hindsight and some previously untapped recollections from people involved. The present-day *Daily Mirror* management graciously consented to the original material being recycled and I have cleaned up the worst failings of structure and syntax that marred the first version, rectified some minor factual errors and inserted a few clarifications of time and place. What follows, though, remains a period piece. To anyone reading the story now who thinks it ill-written, badly constructed, sensationalised and in seriously bad taste I can only say – you should have seen it before.

Anthony Delano 2009

– 1 –

The face is unforgettable. Heart-shaped. A little lacking in chin that, together with the too-high forehead, kept it on the losing side of beautiful. But a perky face; all-American, tipped-up, cheerleader nose. Big brown eyes, velvety with appeal and promise. The upper lip is a little thin and peevish. But the lower is curved, shiny, sensual. An eager mouth; grinning, it spreads into a wide crescent, moist, mushy and crimson as a slice of watermelon.

The face is in constant motion. It has a whole vocabulary of smiles, pouts and puckers; of nose wrinkling, lash fluttering, eye swirling. Especially for men. Young men. The more experienced pick up the scent of trouble.

The sound effects are memorable too. Endearing giggles. The syrupy, enticing accent of the Middle South. A way of speaking that leaves statements suspended breathlessly on the hook of a question mark. Often the voice would take on a querulous edge. How could the whole world misjudge such a natural, well-meaning, God-fearing young woman only out to claim the love, happiness and fulfilment that was hers by right? Or, if she could not have that love, then the glamour and acclaim for which she always knew she was destined? Sooner or later Joyce would tell everyone she met, 'One day I'm going to be famous...'

Joyce McKinney, whose face and voice this is, made a way of life out of altering her looks. The make-up case that she always carried with her – into action, into prison, into hiding – was a magic box, a sorcerer's paraphernalia with which she tried time and again, behind many faces and names, to transform her achingly frustrating life.

Sometimes she succeeded briefly – once spectacularly –

pulling a chair out from under the staid British legal establishment just as it was about to sit in ponderous judgment on her. On the run in Canada and back home in the United States, she relied on the magic make-up kit to keep her a jump ahead of the patient computers of the FBI.

Sometimes the voice was all belle-like sighs and self-pity. 'Ah *craaaaahhed...*' Joyce would breathe, telling how she had wept over some of the things that had happened in her life up to the incandescent notoriety she won for herself in Britain. 'Ah never knew that people could be so *crewwuhl.*'

But then, many people could never imagine that the real world held anyone like Joyce. Someone who for love – of a very odd lover – would be, in her own immortal words, '...prepared to ski naked down Mount Everest with a carnation up my nose.'

Joyce McKinney deserved her moment of outrageous fame. She accomplished something quite unprecedented either in the annals of British justice or of Women's Liberation. She was accused of kidnapping a young Mormon missionary she had followed to Britain from the United States. She made a legend of herself by hounding down that beefy young religious zealot who had come (with some reason) to regard her as an Imp of Satan, snaring him with wiles worthy of Wonder Woman and then Having Her Way with him. If a man had treated Joy as she had treated her reluctant lover the charge against him would undoubtedly have been rape. As a definition of what makes news, Woman Ravishes Man has it all over Man Bites Dog.

Even after that spectacular escapade Joyce managed to project and promote an image of outraged maidenhood. Apart from the voice and the watermelon grin the most noticeable things about Joy (as she preferred to be called – 'You know, *Joy to the World* – the Christmas carol') were her cascade of blonde hair and her aggressively self-supporting bosom. Both of these, she would emphasise, even to a recent acquaintance, were entirely genuine. Nothing in the least artificial, was her proud boast. Like most of Joy's assertions about herself, that was about half true.

The golden locks curled over to hide a scar on the right side of

Joy's jaw. She would fiddle endlessly with her artfully cut hair making sure it stayed in place. That flaw on her face embarrassed her. But had she not acquired it in the way she did, the international soap opera that rocketed her to stardom might never have got off its launching pad.

The bosom, however, the prime '38-inch C-cup' statistics on which Joy had relied so much in her beauty-contest days, was rarely concealed entirely, even in public. One or another of the impressive twin assets would often escape from their flimsy restraints, causing consternation to onlookers although never to Joy.

By the time Joy propelled herself explosively on to the world's front pages, the rest of the statistics that had taken her within tantalisingly close reach of a beauty queen's crown were no longer quite what they once had been. At the age of exactly 28 – on August 6, 1977 – her hips had spread a little wider than the 36 inches she was proud of back in 1975. Nor did she seem to be quite the willowy five-foot, seven-inches tall that she claimed on her resumé; in fact (as one of the good-old-boys of her North Carolina past might have said) her ass was a mite close to the ground.

Looks may have let Joy down in the glamour market but they were perfectly adequate for the acting career she had studied for. She was smart enough. A Master of Arts, although not, as she was fond of claiming, a Doctor of Philosophy. And she was no quitter – as millions of entranced Britons were to find out – more than ready to match wiles with the secretive and powerful Church of Latter Day Saints, the Mormons.

Since her charms had proved wanting in the first bid she made to achieve celebrity by zeroing in on Wayne Osmond, of the ever-smiling, invincibly virtuous, clan of singing Mormons, she set out to improve them. By the time she arrived in Britain to collect the truly bizarre debt she considered she was owed as a consequence of the second serious marriage prospect to have eluded her, Joy had trained herself to be a skilled and enthusiastic exponent of the erotic arts.

Her powers as an actress had also developed. Right up until she was about to go on trial at the Old Bailey she had the country at large convinced that she was the victim in the case rather than the villain. And when the debaucheries of her past were on the point of being revealed by a newspaper investigation and the spotlight in which she revelled suddenly generated more heat than she could bear, Joy, ingeniously disguised, brought down the curtain with a spectacular exit.

– 2 –

Millions of Britons who had been grateful for the warmth Joy brought into their lives that winter felt thoroughly deprived on May 2, 1978, when she and her inseparable accomplice, Keith May, failed to show up for their trial. It had promised to be a marvellous show. In the grim setting of the Central Criminal Court – to give the Old Bailey its proper name – Joy would have sparkled like a gaudy, if flawed, jewel.

The only regret in the mind of anyone with an enlightened interest in the case was that the show would have only a brief run. Joy seemed certain to be acquitted. There was widespread surprise that she was being tried at all; that £100,000 or so of public money was being spent to argue over the fine points of a splendidly un-English erotic charade. But Joy's many fans were looking forward to seeing her in action again, however fleetingly, and the trial, had it taken place, would have given them their first good look at the enigmatic man at the centre of the case.

That was not Keith, who faced charges as portentous as those against Joy. He was an intriguing enough figure, the unlucky one among a kind of suicide squad of young men that Joy had managed to bend to her will. Britain was waiting to see more than the little they had so far been shown of the juvenile lead in this irresistible farce: Kirk Anderson of the pious hamlet of Orem, Utah, trombone player, apple of his mother's eye and Elder of the Melchizedek Priesthood of the Mormon Church who had, since his first tantalising appearance, been kept well out of the public eye.

Joy and Keith had been released from the more stringent restrictions on their movements imposed by the magistrates who with some reluctance – justified as it turned out – had eventually allowed them bail. The melon grin became a familiar sight around London as Joy harvested the luscious fruits of fame. The public soon heard of the claims the couple made to be enjoying a platonic relationship, even though they lived together – had to, as a condition of their bail – but only the relatively few people who had come to know the two young Americans at first hand realised how utterly blind Keith was with love for Joy. When she spoke he began or finished her sentences. Fell in with her every like and dislike, whether of food, people or prayer. Cut Joy, Keith bled.

It was Kirk Anderson, shielded for months by the Elders of his church, to whom Joy claimed she had surrendered her virginity; the man she said had fathered the unborn child she claimed to have lost; the man by whom she had intended to become pregnant again – whether he liked the process or not. Kirk was to have been the chief prosecution witness – the only one, really – in the case of the Queen v. Joyce McKinney.

The Old Bailey was a mere stone's throw from the offices of the *Daily Mirror*, Britain's archetypal tabloid. On the day the names of Joyce and Keith went unanswered when an usher called them out the traditional thrice the editor of the *Mirror*, Michael Molloy, could cheerfully have heaved a brick at the gilded figure of Justice topping the court's elegant dome. The same went for the paper's only woman executive, assistant editor Joyce Hopkirk, and for its news editor, Alan Shillum. They all spent a good part of the day feeling painfully mocked by the sight of the golden lady with the scales at the centre of the panoramic view from Molloy's window.

Waiting outside the Bailey that morning were the *Mirror's* top photographer, Kent Gavin, and two energetic reporters, Barry Wigmore and Roger Beam, all of whom had a burning interest in the case. Gradually they accepted the worst: the two defendants had jumped bail and in all probability fled the country. Conversations with the senior police officers and the barristers who had put in a formal appearance in case, against all odds, Joy, or some word from her, arrived, confirmed the *Mirror*

13

men's worst fears: ponderous legalities meant there was no way, at least for the moment, that the newspaper would be able to tell the astonishing truth it had learnt about Joyce McKinney.

It was a catastrophe. The *Mirror* was girding up for a circulation battle with its closest rival, the *Sun*. Every popular newspaper had seen advertising revenue suffer in the grim economic slump developing in the late 1970s and the scoop on which the *Mirror* had been sitting for weeks would have sold hundreds of thousands of additional copies. Explosive television commercials had been made and at least £250,000 committed to broadcasting them once Joyce's fate was settled. Now, it seemed, everything might have to wait until the defendants were found and every passing day made it more likely that the *Mirror*'s precarious exclusive would leak away. But all the lawyers were adamant. Any disclosures likely to influence jurors in a future trial would be contempt of court. The editor of a newspaper that published them could go to prison.

At 37, Molloy was the youngest editor of a British national paper for many years. Since taking the job he had been battling to keep circulation well ahead of the other three tabloids that had, of late, come barking down Fleet Street at the heels of the *Mirror*.

The *Daily Mail* and the *Daily Express* were a threat only to each other. But Molloy knew that the *Sun*, helped by industrial difficulties that had recently gnawed at the *Mirror* circulation, was getting ready to claim a two per cent lead. The frustration was all the more acute because in the journalists' view the story that lay locked in Molloy's safe, in thick evenly typed dossiers and folders full of pictures, had no bearing on whether Joy was guilty or innocent of the charge of kidnapping. It was far more sensational than that. Molloy had a fondness for military metaphors. 'I feel,' he said to the others who shared his frustration, 'as Harry Truman might if he had been given the atom bomb at the end of World War II and didn't have a plane to drop it from.'

For the moment the *Mirror*, like its competitors, had to make do with the story of Joy's sudden departure from the country upon which she had descended so explosively nine months earlier. The army of reporters assigned to the task soon discovered that she had fled Britain, just as she had come, on a false passport. In typical fashion, Joy had cultivated a helper for such an occasion, should it arise: Annette Thatcher, landlady of the boarding house in which Joy and Keith lived before the judge who renewed their bail allowed them to rent a house.

Conspiratorial as always, Joy had lured Annette into her service, encouraging her with whisky for which, as Annette was later to admit, she had a weakness. In the pubs where the two women and Keith plotted, certain that their house had been bugged by the Mormons she feared so much, Joy herself drank only orange juice. In their scheming phone calls Joy insisted that Annette call her by a teenage nickname of which she was singularly proud – Iceberg.

The *Mirror* made the best of one advantage it had: a set of Polaroid pictures of the fugitives in disguise, and the documents they had used to get their phoney passports. Roger Beam, a favourite of Joy's because she thought he looked something like her Kirk, got his hands on the material in circumstances he was never ready to disclose. That made a splendid front page but it may also have contributed to the agonising stalemate that ensued. The Director of Public Prosecutions, made to look foolish at having lost the suspects, doggedly refused to say whether there was going to be an attempt to extradite them from wherever they might be found.

Within a few days, however, brief calls began to come in – charges reversed – from Joy and Keith in the United States. Secrets rarely lasted long in Fleet Street, where the offices of the national titles were only a few minutes stroll apart and journalists from all of them mingled in the pubs. But the story proved watertight and, eventually, the *Mirror* team realised that without their having to make a move a trap was setting itself into which one of their rivals might easily fall. Three nail-biting weeks later it was not the *Sun* that took the bait but the *Daily Express*, by 'finding' Joyce and Keith in Atlanta, Georgia, and buying up her story for a whacking £40,000.

15

The set-up was perfect. With deep gratitude for such help in setting the stage, Molloy defied the *Mirror*'s own lawyers and dropped his bomb. The fallout kept Britain laughing for days. It was a brutal scoop. The deodorised old rubbish about her life that Joyce unloaded on the *Express* was swept away overnight by the story that rolled off the *Mirror* presses at the same time; a story no rival paper had even guessed at. A story of ambition, delusion, of thwarted love. Of gratitude. Of religious folly, money, conspiracy, fashionable perversion. But, above all, of a truly remarkable obsession.

– 3 –

British newspaper readers heard of Joy's alleged victim before they heard of her. The stories that appeared in the editions of September 15, 1977, a Thursday, were quite informative considering the difficulty reporters in Britain have in getting any reliable information at all from the police; but only moderately intriguing. A young Mormon missionary, Kirk Anderson, 21, appeared to have been kidnapped from outside his church in East Ewell, near Kingston-upon-Thames, by a man calling himself Bob Bosler.

'We are very alarmed about Mr Anderson's fate,' said the familiar anonymous spokesman of Scotland Yard's news bureau. 'We are treating it as a case of abduction and every step is being taken to find out what has happened to him.' The Yard announced that the usual precautions had been applied at ports and airports in case an attempt should be made to take Anderson out of Britain. Most of the details appeared to have come from Anderson's fellow Mormons who had alerted the police. Especially from the companion with whom he had shared digs in Milton Gardens, Epsom, another 21-year old missionary, Kimball Smith.

Young American Mormons doing the traditional stint of missionary duty abroad that their church requires had become a common sight in Britain in recent years and the natives had become quite used to their quaint ways. They moved about in pairs, presumably to provide moral reinforcement against temptation. They were pledged to celibacy and not allowed, for example, to go within arm's length of a presentable female.

In an age of terrorism a reporter's first thoughts upon hearing of a kidnapping naturally turned to the PLO or the IRA. But it was soon to become clear in this case that the Mormons had a pretty good idea of what must have happened to Kirk. Mr Smith had described a meeting with 'Bosler' – Keith May, as it transpired – who had telephoned some days earlier, saying that he was interested in becoming a convert.

The young missionaries must have been thrilled by the call. Easy catches were rare. They were understandably keen to get their man around to the local Mormon headquarters as soon as possible, following the rendezvous with him that they arranged at the church on Wednesday, September 14. As Smith told it to the police, Kirk and 'Bosler' went to a car outside the church to look up the way on a map. They never came back.

Right away, the Mormons told the police that Kirk, who had been in Britain for ten months, had been the victim of conspicuous harassment before he left Utah. Windows had been smashed at his home, his car run off the road. But at first, apparently, the Mormons did not suggest who might have been responsible.

There was a heavy news schedule at the *Mirror* that Wednesday night. A tabloid newspaper can never find room for every story available on a given day and this one got short shrift. A couple of pages of copy on the first known facts had been telephoned in by a district correspondent or 'stringer' but the news-desk copytaster, the man who winnows the flow of stories, saw that a missing Mormon did not stand much chance of making the paper. Mormons sounded like the kind of religious oddballs to whom internal strife and squabble was endemic. Such a 'kidnapping' would probably turn out to be something rather less interesting. The copytaster reached for his wire spike, the most ancient item of equipment in a modern newspaper office after the pencils, and impaled the stringer's story.

Most other papers also spiked it or reduced it to a couple of insignificant paragraphs.

By Saturday, however, things were a little different. Sunday papers have more space than their daily counterparts, but the stories they carry are of necessity about matters of no particular immediacy. Sunday paper news editors pine for a 'hard' news story to break. On September 17 they got one.

The *Sunday Times:* 'The Mormon missionary missing in Surrey turned up yesterday and said he had been kidnapped and held handcuffed and manacled for three days on the orders of a wealthy lovesick woman.'

News of the World: 'A police chief said the motive could be summed up in the phrase: 'Hell hath no fury like a woman scorned!'

Wealthy... lovesick... woman scorned... this was something else.

On Sunday, always a thin time for daily papers, the *Mirror* knew where it stood. Alan Shillum had already been briefed on the Sunday paper investigations by his man on Saturday duty in the *Mirror* office. When Ron Ricketts, one of the veterans of the *Mirror* newsgathering staff, came into the office on Sunday morning he found himself assigned to Epsom police station, where Kirk was recovering from his ordeal as a guest of the local police.

Ricketts was pleased to be given a story that he could go out and do rather than spend Sunday with a telephone pressed to his ear, an all-too frequent fate when time is short and not enough reporters are on duty. Usually there would be only two reasons to send a reporter to Epsom – Royal Epsom as it enjoys being styled because of the interest taken in it by the British monarchy at least once a year: the Derby and the Oaks, two great horse races named after Lord Derby and his estate, take place there. The last time Ricketts had been out that way he got a rather good story. Lord Wigg, the supremo of British turf events, had gone down to try to persuade the gypsies who traditionally congregate on Epsom Downs during Derby Week from putting in an appearance that year. In the wrangle that ensued, the gipsy leaders had been disarmed by Wigg's revelation, subsequently headlined, that he had some Romany blood in his veins.

The recollection of that little triumph made Ricketts feel quite optimistic, His first objective, the obvious move in such cases, was to visit the victim's home. There was usually more information to be got from relatives than from the police; family snaps to be 'collected' from the mantelpiece, for example. Neighbours to be skilfully led into indiscretions.

It took him a while to find Milton Gardens, a newly built close of town-houses. The one in which Kirk and Smith had lived was hard to miss. A milkman pointed to the huge cluster of milk bottles at the door. The devout Mormons, forbidden tea, coffee, alcohol and even, strictly speaking, Coke, were his best customers.

There was no one home. The neighbours knew very little of the young missionaries. They went out early each morning to their harvesting of souls and returned late at night. Ricketts mooched off to the police station without much hope of gleaning more than the barest details, and it was as well that he did. Just leaving, was a tall and imposing American: Richard Eyre, director of the Southern Region of the Mormon Church in Britain. Under the assumption that the reporters must already know it, he let slip something vital. The person suspected of kidnapping Kirk, he said, was called Joyce McKinney. He even spelled out the name. He would say little more though, except that his young acolyte's predicament stemmed from a 'personal problem'.

The British police have two grounds on which to justify their refusal to disclose information about an investigation in progress. One is the archaic and repressive Official Secrets Act. Usually, though, they prefer to base their traditional lack of candour with the press by citing the legal prohibitions against the publication of material relating to accused person who may be going to face trial.

Reporters find this deeply galling. They hardly need reminding by the police of the limits within which newspapers are forced to operate. These, however, are not set by the police but by Parliament and the courts. Journalists see no reason why the police should not give them information and let them or their editors decide what use could be made of it and when. So they tend, rather surlily, to the belief that the police simply think that no one but themselves has the right to enquire into misdeeds.

But policemen are human. So, even, are lawyers. Reporters soon learn the workings of the delicate mechanism by which a few scrapings can be gleaned of matters that ought not to be made public until they are disclosed in court: the golden rule of 'You never heard it from me'.

Ricketts, chatting assiduously to detectives and uniformed coppers around the Epsom nick, discovered that in addition to Kirk several other men (but no women) were, in the hallowed official formula, 'helping the police with their enquiries'. Joyce McKinney, whoever and whatever she was, seemed still to be at large.

Good. That meant a search. With a suspect in custody the press would, in effect, have been muzzled. Only in recent years have British newspapers been able even to name a person suspected of a crime in advance of their being charged. Even then it was only done, generally speaking, if the police requested it, thus, implicitly, accepting the responsibility. A hunt would offer the press some time in which a little speculation or a few factoids about the fugitive might be published without incurring the wrath of the Attorney General.

So when the dozen or so reporters from national dailies, television and radio jammed into a tiny room on the first floor of Epsom police station there was not much in the way of pressure that they could apply. They were dependent for more information on the man in charge of the investigation, Detective Chief Superintendent Bill Hucklesby.

Hucklesby did not look like an average copper. He was an impressive, fit-looking, well-dressed man in his 40s with a rather soldierly air. Ricketts, who had done some time in Northern Ireland, thought he looked more like a major of commandos.

Hucklesby was certainly smart enough to realise that if he wanted the press to help spread a net for the people he was looking for, it might be a good idea to offer something to whet the reporters' appetite. Just letting it be known that the men he had in custody were not Americans and that their involvement in the investigation seemed to be slight was not very appetising. Nothing very exciting, either, about the beige Ford Cortina, licence number TPK761S found abandoned in London and connected to the events.

So Hucklesby went ahead and named names: Keith Joseph May, aged 24, five foot ten inches, sandy-coloured hair streaked with blonde, believed to be wearing jeans and a knitted cap. Also known as – or as the police in Keith's native California would have said *aka* – Bob Bosler and Paul Van Deusen. Believed to be travelling with the female suspect, Joyce McKinney, as man and wife.

However, it was the names that the female suspect appeared to be aka that made the reporters lick their lips as they scribbled. In addition to Mrs Bosler, Joyce was Kathie Vaughn Bare, Cathy Van Deusen and Heidi Krazler. The description that followed was nearly as exotic as those akas. Long blonde hair and armed with a collection of wigs of various hue. A pronounced Southern accent. There were also intriguing flaws in the fantasy image coalescing in the newsmen's minds. Triangular scar on jaw. Wire-rimmed spectacles with very thick lenses.

Something that was indispensable to a robust tabloid account needed to be established. 'Chief Superintendent,' asked Ricketts, 'Would you say this young woman could be called *attractive?*'

'Oh yes,' said Hucklesby. 'Very!' The reporters were delighted. The photographers and cameramen disgusted. They could not take a picture of a description.

More questions. Were the charges being contemplated against whatever-her-real-name-is serious? 'Kidnapping is always a serious offence,' said Hucklesby firmly. 'Serious allegations have been made.'

Ricketts had enough for the moment. The story had wings. He telephoned the *Mirror* and dictated to a copy-taker: 'Police tonight named a beautiful American woman as the ...' This time the story went in the paper. So did the stories that he and other reporters filed the following day. Joy and Keith were arrested in their hired car at a police roadblock on the road back from Devon to London. Without the aid of the press.

Hucklesby was ecstatic. 'They have been detained as the result of a massive exercise in cooperation with the Devon and Cornwall Constabulary,' he said. 'They fell into a police trap.' To a considerably enlarged audience of reporters he confided that the Yard had used the situation to rehearse police reaction to a terrorist political kidnapping, should such a thing ever occur in Britain.

Back in London, more reporters were making transatlantic telephone calls, tracking down Kirk's home in Utah and Joy's in North Carolina. Marilyn McKinney was more than ready to tell of her daughter's romance with Kirk at Brigham Young University in Utah. 'They talked about getting married,' she said. 'Joyce blames me for trying to break up their love affair because I didn't like the Mormon Church. Joyce is an introvert and a terribly lonely person.'

Kirk's mother was a good deal less candid. 'We didn't know anything about this girl,' said Barbara Anderson. 'We do know he's had nothing to do with girls – except to teach them about the church. I personally think he's been living very close to the Lord.'

Other reporters descended on the family that had rented Joy a remote cottage on the northern edge of Dartmoor, near Okehampton, for £50 a week. Searching the place, Detective Chief Superintendent John Bissett from the Surrey CID had found handcuffs and foot manacles that the tenants appeared to have left behind.

News editors compared the copy coming in from all sources, raised their eyebrows slightly and briefed the reporters in Epsom on what had been discovered in the West Country. At the next audience with Hucklesby Ricketts was ready to push his luck while the detective was so pleased with his progress. 'Tell me, Chief Superintendent,' he asked, 'is there supposed to be anything, well... *sexual* about this abduction?'

The stern and serious manner Hucklesby had maintained during the suspenseful few days of the search for Joy and Keith gave way to nonplussed amusement. By then he had interviewed Joy, who had been brought to Epsom under escort. She had been anything but reticent in telling him about what she had done to – or, as she insisted, done *with* – Kirk.

'Off the record,' said Hucklesby (although both he and the

23

reporters were well aware that nothing could be published about matters that might become prosecution evidence), 'this is the most extraordinary case I've ever investigated.'

Ricketts waited nonchalantly.

'All I can say is that we found... er... certain equipment... But I'll tell you what,' Hucklesby added in a burst of fraternal confidence. 'I've never been lucky enough to have anything like that happen to me!' As Keith May was to say when he was out on bail three months later, 'This is a pretty strange country. If Joy had been busted in the US for doing what she did to Kirk the only thing the cops would have done before they let her go was make sure they had her phone number.'

Then and there, however, in the strange country the Epsom reporters were beginning to feel a little uneasy. Ricketts thought he might as well ask the obvious question, even though the answer could only be used for the guidance of his editors. 'Do you think that she will come to trial, then? That she'll be fit to plead?'

'I think she's emotionally unstable,' said Hucklesby.

Unstable or not, Joyce McKinney was fascinating newspaper fodder. But she was still an elusive, unglimpsed figure, hard to bring to life from the lines of terse tabloid prose that piled up beneath the daily headlines. The public needed a look at her.

Thus far, she and Keith had been spotted only momentarily by a couple of newsmen when they arrived at Epsom from Devon in separate police cars in the early hours of the Tuesday morning. Joy wore a beige jumper and trousers. Her hair was a mess, presumably because she had been made to lie down in the back seat of the car, a policewoman covering her face with a jacket.

She begged the police to tell her where Kirk Anderson was. They did not let on that her accuser was in a room just a few doors down the corridor from the one in which she was given a quick medical examination.

Then she was sent off to spend the rest of the night in another police station at distant Tooting.

Hucklesby was taking no chances. Most of the Scotland Yard

officers had the gravest doubts that they could believe anything of the preposterous story they were being told but some still suspected an international plot. Joy's car had yielded two convincing replicas of .38 Colt Detective Special revolvers; a bottle of ether mixed with chloroform; some tapes of soothing music; a complete bridal trousseau, heavy on frillies and baby-doll nighties; and a couple of other little items that caused the stalwarts of the Devon and Cornwall Constabulary to scratch their heads and lick their pencils thoughtfully, as they listed them as evidence.

The following day Joy looked a little better. The police had given her some clothes from her luggage: an uncharacteristically demure green dress, brown coat and white shoes. Once again she had to suffer a blanket being draped over her head by her conscientious escort. The police insist on this tiresome precaution in case a photograph of a suspect might influence jurors or witnesses who would later have to swear to an identification.

That was hardly the case with Joy. She was ready to tell everyone what she had done – and why. She could hardly wait to give her new-found public its first good look at her.

− 4 −

So far, Joy had made a tremendous splash in public print from the British Isles to the Great Smoky Mountains and all points in between. Alas, when she made her court debut at Epsom on September 29 the *Daily Mirror* could do nothing about it. A smouldering dispute between the paper's management and the National Union of Journalists – instead of, as more commonly, the printers – had flared into a bad-tempered confrontation that prevented the paper from coming out that day. Molloy and those of his staff whose newshound instincts were unimpaired by the efforts their colleagues were making for more pay pored ravenously over the accounts in opposition papers of how Joy had smuggled a message to reporters past the coppers escorting her to her first brief magistrates' court appearance. 'I am innocent,' her note said. 'Please help me.'

What a day to miss publication, dammit!

Joy and Keith were remanded in custody – returned to jail until their next court appearance. Chapter and verse of the alleged kidnapping of Kirk had been spelled out in solemn legal language: forcibly abducting, assaulting and unlawfully imprisoning him. In addition, the pair were accused of possessing imitation revolvers 'with intent to commit an offence'. Since they had now been formally charged, the restrictions intended to protect future jurors from prejudice cut them off from the public like a soundproof barrier.

Newsroom activity, however, went into high gear. It remained to be seen what evidence the police had to offer that could convince the magistrates that Joy and Keith deserved to be sent to trial at the Old Bailey. There had been only hints of what the pair might eventually say in their defence but it was apparent to the popular tabloids that a much more detailed story would remain to be told after their trial. Or once the charges had been dismissed, which even at that stage seemed a strong possibility. With the future in mind, Shillum and his rival Fleet Street news editors mobilised correspondents in the United States to begin preparing dossiers on the background of Joy and Keith.

The *Mirror* reporter assigned to Epsom Court for Joy's next scheduled appearance, a technical 'pop-up' on the following Thursday, October 6, was Garth Gibbs, a South African with an amiable, deceptively world-weary manner. He could be fast on his feet when he needed to. This was to be one of those days.

Joy was about to give a useful hint of her future intentions; of the astuteness she was to show so abundantly in the future when it came to getting herself the best press possible. By then she had spent 19 days in Holloway, London's miserable and decrepit prison for women. As a prisoner on remand she was allowed to read as many papers as she wished. She studied them all carefully. Once she grasped what they wanted she knew how to give it to them. Britain's tabloids, with their heavy emphasis on human interest stories, were made for the likes of Joy. And, as their readers were soon to see, she was made for the tabs.

Joy also read her Bible regularly like the good Christian girl she insisted to everyone that she was, especially to the Holloway lesbians who, she complained to her bewildered mother and father, who had arrived from North Carolina to be at the side of their only child, just *would* not leave her alone. She made sure to take the Bible with her when she got into a Black Maria to be driven down to Epsom. She sat quietly until the van backed up to the door through which she was to enter the court and as soon as she spotted the unruly pack of reporters and photographers about 25 yards away, the police holding them back, she flew into action.

She opened the Good Book, held it up to the barred window of the van and began wailing for attention. Gibbs bolted through the police line to get close enough to read Joy's message to the world.

'Please tell the truth,' she had scribbled across the pages of the Book of Job. 'My reputation is at stake.'

Gibbs would do his best that day to tell as much as he could; but the truth about Joy McKinney was to be a long while coming.

A woman prison officer in the van struggled to pull her away from the window but the furious activity of the photographers outside encouraged Joy to crank up her performance. Clinging to the Bible she opened it again at the Gospel According to Saint Mark. There she had scrawled, 'He had sex with me for four days'.

Goggle-eyed and grateful, Gibbs repeated the words to himself, memorising them. While the guard desperately tried to tear the Bible away from her, Joy turned to yet another page: 'Please get the truth to the public. He made it look like a kidnapping.' And on yet another: 'Ask Christians to pray for me.' Gibbs was already uttering silent prayers of gratitude, imagining the scribbles transmuted into front page headlines.

Out of the van, Joy, dressed in a white cheesecloth dress caught at the waist with a green sash, paused to allow the distant cameramen to frame their shots. They were cursing the rainy morning and a range too great for the flash of their strobes to carry. Instantly picking up on the problem, Joy moaned plaintively and made a rush at the press ranks. Hefty police arms caught her – as she had known they must – and she was bundled into the court.

Mirror photographer Alisdair MacDonald, a cool and taciturn craftsman, had been shooting past Gibbs as the reporter craned to read Joy's messages. His lens caught Joy's lunge at just the instant she would have chosen if she had pressed the button herself.

The *Daily Mirror* front page the following day was one of the most striking of the year. But the brief story accompanying the splendid picture of Joy (in her loose and promising neckline) struggling with her minders did not include the phrase about Kirk having sex with her. Nor the one about 'making it look like a kidnap'. Those were references to matters that would have to be decided by the courts and *Mirror* lawyers would not allow them to be used.

Gibbs and Joy were equally chagrined.

That time, Joy and Keith were in court for a mere two minutes. But at their appearance the following Thursday, October 12, they were ready to apply for bail. Some of the vagaries of the British legal system had been patiently explained to Joy by her court-appointed solicitor Stuart Elgrod. In preliminary hearings of this kind the press were restricted to publishing only the names, ages and addresses of the accused and the formal details of the charges. They would not be able to report the evidence given by either side.

Not able to print what she planned to say in court? Joy was appalled. Not, said Elgrod, unless she exercised her right to ask for the reporting restrictions to be lifted, a course he would not advise. Elgrod, a young local solicitor, still had a lot to learn about his intriguing new client. They applied for the restrictions to be lifted.

Fleet Street was duly thankful, even though the most interesting disclosure that day was about the fake passports Joy and Keith had used to enter Britain. He possessed documents in nine different names. She in a mere four. Joy was described as a 'model', a tired label that made the reporters roll their eyes. Keith was said to be a trainee architect. Elgrod argued strongly for Joy to be released on bail. Whatever happened to Kirk Anderson, he said, had been not merely with the consent of the young Mormon but, on occasion, at his instigation. Kirk, said Elgrod, had neither been taken away against his wishes nor kept away.

Chief Superintendent Hucklesby appeared in person to oppose bail. Keith May was a pilot, he said, implying that he might fly himself away. Joy had made suicide attempts in the past – something the reporters were hearing about for the first time. The magistrates were asked to conclude that she might do herself in. Hucklesby won.

He won again a week later when his prisoners repeated their application. On that occasion the solicitor representing Joy – an associate of Elgrod, Anthony Edwards – did the press a good turn by offering an explanation for Joy's collection of false identities: she lived in terror of the Mormons.

'She was converted to the Mormon faith but became disillusioned with it,' he told the magistrates. 'She is very much afraid of the retribution that the Mormons will take on her for going back on her conversion. More so, because she tried to see a missionary who at this stage should not have been associating with women.'

As on each of her previous three appearances, Joy sobbed and pleaded with the newsmen covered the proceedings. That was no more than they had come to expect of her. The audience Joy had created for herself needed more. Editorial attention turned toward the enigmatic and intriguing Mormons.

– 5 –

In Britain there had only ever been a few mentions of Kirk's birthplace, Orem, Utah, as the home of the Osmond Family, the multi-Mormon showbiz tribe, and of superstar Robert Redford. Joy now turned it into an international dateline.

Delicate behind-the-scenes give and take among reporters, detectives and solicitors at Epsom suggested that the suicide attempt that had been mentioned in court with such tantalising brevity was caused – according to Joy – by a disastrous romance with Wayne Osmond.

Telephone enquiries from London turned up a link. Olive Osmond, the formidable matriarch of the clan, insisted it was a link of the most tenuous kind. 'I can say categorically she has never dated my boys,' said Mrs. Osmond, righteously, to those who phoned her.

'I know Joyce McKinney and I talked to her just as much as the boys did. We were aware of her, because for a time she was always there. She is an extremely beautiful, intelligent girl. But we never regarded her as anything special. As far as we are concerned, she is just another of their fans.'

Nothing special? The words would have pierced Joy's heart.

Mrs Osmond deplored the lengths to which some girls would go to make a connection with her clean-cut lads. 'Some of them are absolutely unbelievably forward. They would break down barriers and push through walls to get their hands on my boys. It's a fight all the time, keeping them at arm's length.'

All the reporters on the other end of this and similar conversations with Mrs Osmond felt she might be protesting a little too much. 'I know my boys better than anyone. They are strong and disciplined. None of them would date any girl they just met casually.' Joy had hardly met the Osmonds casually.

She had been as methodical about infiltrating their privileged ranks at the core of the closed and infinitely discreet Mormon community as she had been about all the compulsions that periodically took over her life.

Christopher Buckland, the *Mirror*'s Washington correspondent, went to Avery County, North Carolina, where Joy had spent her childhood in the village of Minneapolis. Her father, David, 48, still ran the elementary school where as a glaringly untypical young schoolgirl his daughter had shown the first signs of the insatiable appetite for attention and adulation that were to drive her to such excesses a few years later.

Buckland could not unearth many recent memories. They had not seen Joy in Avery County lately, although the folks there had always been kept informed of her progress. Each and every one of the modest triumphs of her lifetime had been faithfully reported back to the local paper, the weekly *Avery Journal,* by Joy herself. The first clipping in the *Journal* files, from early 1973, fairly breathed accomplishment:

> Miss Joy McKinney has won the leading role of Amanda Wingfield in Tennessee Williams's *The Glass Menagerie*, being produced at Brigham Young University in Provo, Utah, June 8-16.
>
> The daughter of Mr. and Mrs. D L McKinney of Minneapolis, Joy attended Cranberry High School and graduated in 1967.
>
> Presently working on her doctorate at Brigham Young, Joy received her BA degree from East Tennessee State and her MA from the University of North Carolina. While at BYU she is on a graduate assistanceship program teaching classes in speech. Working at the University of Tennessee, Miss McKinney produced and hosted a television special entitled *The Scrapbook: An Historical Documentary Commemorating Twenty Years of Carousel Theatre*, a joint university-community venture in Knoxville, Tenn. And for her master's thesis, she worked with the Knoxville Police Department in writing *Diary of a Drug Addict*, a dramatic vignette involving the adaptation of the drug problem in Knoxville to a television documentary drama.

By 1974 the emphasis of Joy's activities had shifted from good works to glamour. Buckland soon realised that he was assembling a disturbing portrait of a young woman falling under the sway of her earliest delusion; the conviction that she was an irresistible beauty.

'BYU Co-ed headed for contest,' said a *Journal* headline. The dusty old term 'co-ed' for a girl student lived on in Avery County. There were pictures of Joy in queenly poses. In cheery small-town paper style the caption – clearly provided by Joy – read:

> Miss Joyce McKinney, a coed at Brigham Young University, is in New York this week representing Wyoming in the Miss USA contest. ABC will carry the pageant September 25. Bob Hope will emcee the affair. Miss McKinney was chosen in the Western states division contest which included girls from Utah, Wyoming, Idaho and Colorado. The daughter of Mr and Mrs D L McKinney of Newland and the granddaughter of Mrs Lige Smith of Minneapolis, Joy is working toward her doctorate at Brigham Young in theatre work.

Buckland found the whole county reeling from the impact of Joy's recent performance. Reports of it had been running in the *Journal* as a weekly serial. One instalment described Epsom as 'a small village near London,' which was hardly the way it would describe itself. Avery County should talk. It is hillbilly country, half the size of Surrey.

North Carolina was the site of Walter Raleigh's first attempt to establish a colony in the New World. The people of the Appalachian Mountains – Joy's people – are of the earliest English and Scottish stock, singing songs and speaking dialect that would hardly be understood in their great-great grandmother countries, stubborn, independent, isolated, godly. Violent, too. There were only 13,000 people in the entire county but the issue of the *Journal* that brought the astounding news of Joy's predicament also carried stories of a shotgun duel and a traffic contretemps that ended in a stabbing. In addition there was a photograph of 'Mrs Margaret Thatcher, leader of the British Conservation Party'.

Buckland saw a lot of Avery County on his rounds. It is gorgeous countryside, rich with red spruce and yellow birch towering over hundreds of kinds of flowering shrubs. The summers are steamy and the winters chill, hinting still of one of the great crimes of American history. The notorious Trail of Tears began in the nearby Great Smoky Mountains, along which, more than a century ago, the US Army drove the Cherokee Indians from their ancient home to exile in Oklahoma.

He talked to a lot of people who remembered Joy. Brenda Gardner, a clerk in the County Offices in the town of Newland, had shared a desk with her at Cranberry High. 'She was always the brightest girl in class. Straight A's in all her subjects,' she told him. 'I never recall her dating much back then.'

Back then was nine years earlier. What Brenda remembered best about Joy was 'just how nice she was'.

Same with Ivan Hoilman, another of Joy's contemporaries, now a detective in the local police force. 'Joy used to be a bit skinny,' Ivan reminisced. 'But she sure was a real blonde bombshell. She became a drum majorette and a cheerleader too. She was an only child so I reckon she was a bit spoiled. She was always the best-dressed girl in school, that I recall. And with her dad a school principal and her ma a teacher, I think some of us kids were just a mite jealous.'

In true country fashion, some of that envy had lingered on. Quite a few people in the county were sourly pleased to see Joy receive such a spectacular come-uppance. 'Of course it's the talk of the county what's been happening over in England', said Ivan. 'We just can't reckon it at all. But me being a detective, well you don't get surprised by anything after a while.'

In the Toe River Valley, the McKinney's fine, single-storey house stood empty and silent. Before the McKinneys left for London, Marilyn had confided in her friends about Joy's disappointments with the only two men she had been in love with. She mentioned that in November 1974, when Wayne Osmond announced his engagement to someone else, Joy had ended up in hospital with emotional problems.

Marilyn thought Kirk Anderson had given her daughter 'a dirty deal' by sloping off after he had spoken of love – and even gone house-hunting with her. She had worried how badly Joy would take to being spurned for a second time. She did not seem to have told anyone in Avery County what really happened to Joy after she lost Kirk.

Buckland caught a train – he was a train freak – back to Washington feeling distinctly thwarted. He knew he might have been able to do a good deal better if only he had been able to employ one of a reporter's most dependable tools and buy some of his contacts a drink. But Avery County was 'dry', the only hard likker bootleg moonshine.

It might also have been helpful if he had known what questions he should have been asking. Although back in Britain, the home side reporters were only just beginning to suspect how much there might be to find out about Joy. However the relationships Buckland established in Avery County stayed fruitful. When, after the details of her encounters of Kirk had been disclosed, Joy wrote a fascinating letter to the *Journal* the paper decided not to publish it. Buckland, however, received a photocopy in the mail. It warned against British snoopers – like himself:

> I urge you to tell them the truth. That my nickname in high school was 'Iceberg'; that I was boy-shy, and seldom dated. (I was more the studious type.) And didn't even play kissing games at parties. Also that I was never known to smoke, drink or use any type of drugs or profanity and that I come from a very good family. Also that I represented Avery County in the Miss North Carolina High School Contest as 'North Carolina's ideal high school girl', as well as being a North Carolina Junior Miss and later Miss Wyoming in the 'Miss USA Pageant'.

Beauty battle honours had come to mean more to Joy than her two college degrees. She listed every pathetic one of them in a detailed resumé she had put out in 1976:

> Chosen as 'private Sweetheart', most photogenic girl in East Tenn. State Univ.
> Chosen Pepsi-Cola Calendar Girl in Johnson City, Tenn.
> Chosen as 'Kappa Alpha Sweetheart' for Kappa Alpha Fraternity.
> Chosen as 'Freshman Beauty' for Univ of North Carolina.
> Chosen as 'Belle of Y' finalist in 1974 Homecoming Queen Contest.
> Selected as model to represent North Carolina Press Photography Pageant for Charlotte, North Carolina.

Only when these precious distinctions had been registered did Joy mention that she was eligible to join Mensa, which she described as the society for people whose intelligence quotient was 'above genius level'.

Joy's parents seemed to have shared her exalted view of herself. It had been made plain to Buckland that the family was far from rich. Marilyn had retired from teaching and was almost crippled with arthritis. Nevertheless, before leaving for Britain she and David raised as much money as they could, assuming that sooner or later Joy would need bail.

At the second Epsom appearance Garth Gibbs had watched the McKinneys carefully as they sat in the public gallery. Marilyn tensed visibly as her daughter was brought up into the dock from the cells below. David leaned forward, straining to hear what was being said. Joy did not glance at either of them. As she was to do on every one of her many court hearings, she snuggled beside Keith May, holding his hand, sometimes resting her head on his shoulder. By then Keith, too, had acquired a Bible to clutch.

Reporters had only been able to speculate among themselves on Keith's relationship to Joy. In applying for bail Keith's counsel, Bob Marshall-Andrews, whose services he had obtained through legal aid, said only that 'mixed-up emotions' were involved. British understatement. It was to be many weeks before Keith would be free and able to explain for himself how he had become ensnared in Joy's plans for Kirk from the very beginning, back in California in 1976.

A budding pilot, he had advertised for flying companions. Joy, in whose life advertisements were to play an overweening part, answered. She explained that she was planning a secret honeymoon. A plane to whisk her and her bridegroom away to some remote paradise might be useful.

After she told Keith something, if not all, about her tortuous romance with Kirk, Keith offered her some advice. 'Give it up,' he said. 'I like you. Let me have a chance.'

'Why does everyone fall in love with me?' asked Joy, voicing another of her persistent delusions.

At the couple's third court appearance a week later Marilyn McKinney gave evidence in support of the bail application. 'There were difficulties between me and my daughter when she became a Mormon,' she said. 'But I am sure these are adequately resolved. I have been visiting my daughter daily at Holloway and she is more and more depressed.'

A whisper from behind Holloway's grimy walls had told of Joy's being passed a £20 note by one of her parents during a kiss. Gibbs felt sorry for Marilyn. Mothers always thought they were responsible for their children's failings. Joy was ready to blame anyone at all for hers.

Anyone but herself.

– 6 –

Soon after Joy's opening performance in court, the *Mirror*'s West Coast correspondent, Jill Evans, left her base in Los Angeles headed for Utah. There, her path would cross the trails of correspondents from other British papers, among them Brian Vine, chief American correspondent of the *Daily Express,* and Philip Finn of the *Daily Mail.* She was pleased to find no trace of anyone from the *Sun.*

Salt Lake City is to the Mormon Church as Canterbury is to the Church of England, the Vatican to Roman Catholics, Mecca to Moslems, Jerusalem to Jews. It is one of the most handsome regional centres in the nation. Its wide tree-lined boulevards march to the cardinal points of the compass in an orderly spread from a centre dominated less by the neo-classic State Capitol than by the religious edifices of Temple Square – which pretty well symbolises the way things are in the state of Utah.

The Square contains two buildings. One is the Tabernacle whose huge elongated wooden dome, sheathed in glinting metal, was built without the use of a single nail. Thousands of tourists visit it each year. Millions everywhere know it as the home of the Mormon Tabernacle Choir, a sort of vocal equivalent to *Come Dancing.* The other building is the Temple itself, to which stream pilgrims from the powerful outposts of the faith at home and abroad. Six spires topping its grey granite walls give it the look of a fairytale stronghold, a touching effigy of a European cathedral built by men who could only imagine what one might look like.

The Tabernacle is open to all. But only worthy Mormons may enter the Temple and join in the sacred and mysterious 'ordinances', ceremonies that unite the living and the dead. The Mormons have many secrets and they guard them well.

From the loftiest of all six Temple spires a gilded angel tilts his trumpet up at the Rocky Mountains. The sun sparkling on it caught Jill Evans's optimistic eye as she headed away from Salt Lake Airport for the town of Provo, driving beside the Union Pacific railroad track where mile-long freight trains still sound their lonely whistle in the sky.

Joy herself had come that same way four years earlier, fired with all the zeal of a recent convert. At university in Tennessee she had, by chance, found 'digs' in a teeming Mormon household. The warm interlocked lives of the children there were so different from her own as an only child that she impulsively decided to convert to become closer to them.

She applied herself to her new religion with the same desperate intensity that went into all her enthusiasms. And when she got a scholarship to Brigham Young University and set out to finish her education in the Mormon heartland she brought with her – in addition to her beloved Old English Sheepdog, Millie – the memory of that embracing, hospitable warmth. She also took along the burdens of her indulgent solitary upbringing, a tiresome Southern-belle self-centredness and impatience; a disturbing inability to accept any viewpoint other than her own.

The Mormon Church, or to give it the title its members prefer, the Church of Jesus Christ of Latter Day Saints, is one of America's most original creations. Its beginnings are probably no more questionable than those of any other religion but since they are, relatively speaking, recent – almost within living memory – they have been sharply scrutinised, especially by more orthodox Christian creeds such as Roman Catholicism and Protestantism, who find that Mormons make unsatisfactory bedfellows. Just as Joy did.

The first LDS was Joseph Smith, a farm boy who claimed that in the year 1820, in a forest glade near the town of Palmyra in New York State, he received a visit from the Lord Jesus Christ and his father, God. He had not been expecting them, Smith later explained. But he *had* been soul-searching about which of the many competing religious persuasions of that time and place he ought to follow.

His visitors advised him against the lot of them, Smith related. 'They were all wrong, and the Personage who addressed me said that all their creeds were an abomination in his sight; that those professors' – those, that is, who professed one faith or another – 'were all corrupt.'

A few years later, on September 21, 1823, to be exact, Smith had another visitation, this time from an angel who introduced himself as Moroni – the golden trumpeter of the Temple spire. According to Moroni, he, Smith, had been chosen to convey the true version of the gospel that had become distorted over the years by the various contending Christian sects.

In due course, confided Moroni, Smith would be vouchsafed a revelation about God's past activities concerning the United States and his plans for its future. The information was already inscribed on golden tablets that lay buried near the Smith home, in a hill that Moroni called Cumorah.

For the next four years Joseph went to Cumorah every September waiting for his instructions. They finally came – delivered by Moroni once again – on September 22, 1827. By his later account, Smith had to lever away the cover of a small stone vault to uncover the tablets. Together with them were two stones set in silver 'bows' that, he was told, were called the Urim and the Thummin.

That description of their shape led detractors of the Mormons to refer to these items as 'the magic spectacles'. Believers insist that they enabled Joseph, a barely literate labourer, to translate the hieroglyphics of 'Reformed Egyptian' in which the story on the tablets was inscribed. The results, dictated by Joe to various friends and acquaintances, became the *Book of Mormon*, the fundamental LDS scripture.

Even at the time not everyone was ready to take the new prophet's word of what had been revealed to him. The Smith family, in which there were nine children, were known to spend much of their time digging for buried treasure. It was not the first time they had told questionable tales. In 1867, by which time the Mormons had become a force to be reckoned with in far-off Utah, a neighbour of the Smiths in their Palmyra days, Pomeroy

Tucker, wrote in a book called *Origin, Rise and Progress of Mormonism*:

> At this period in the life and career of Joseph Smith, or 'Joe Smith' as he was universally named... he is distinctly remembered as a dull, flaxen-haired, prevaricating boy... by reason of the extravagancies of his statement, his word was received with the least confidence by those who knew him best. He could utter the most palpable exaggeration or marvellous absurdity with the utmost apparent gravity.

Earlier, more than 50 residents of Palmyra had put their names to a public disavowal of Smith and his claim in support of one E D Howe, who in 1834 wrote about the Smiths in a book *Mormonism Unveiled*:

> They were particularly famous for visionary projects; spent much of their time in digging for money which they pretended was hidden in the earth, and a large excavation may be seen in the earth not far from their residence where they used to spend their time in digging for hidden treasures. Joseph Smith Sr and his son, Joseph, were particularly considered entirely destitute of moral character and addicted to vicious habits.

No matter. By 1830 the Church of Jesus Christ of Latter Day Saints was proclaimed in Fayette, New York, and with the completed translation of the *Book of Mormon* selling well soon swelled its numbers from six to nearly 600. Every copy of the book bore signed testimony from eleven of the new faithful that they had seen Smith's original golden tablets.

Today's versions still carry the endorsements. However, what these witnesses seem to have meant was that they had been shown the tablets by Moroni in a vision. Or that they had an important qualification to offer, like Martin Harris who financed the printing of the book. 'I did not see them just as I see the penholder,' Harris explained carefully, when pressed about the tablets of gold. 'But I saw them with the eye of faith. Although at the time they were covered over with a cloth.'

Since at Moroni's suggestion the tablets and the 'spectacles' were buried again, no one other than Smith ever did get to see them uncovered. And no one has ever been able to explain 'Reformed Egyptian'.

The central institutions of the Mormon Church became established at the very beginning. Tithing – every Mormon must contribute a tenth of his earnings – and a non-professional clergy. Any faithful and properly instructed Mormon may become, at the age of 12, a member of the Aaronic Priesthood. If he has ambitions to rise in the church hierarchy, however, he must wait until he is 19 and join the Melchisadech Priesthood with its rankings of 'Elders', the oddly-named 'Seventies' and 'High Priests'.

Young Kirk Anderson was a relatively lowly Elder.

The principal beliefs church members must accept were also laid down from the first. The story told in the *Book of Mormon* has a cast of thousands. It begins with the migrations of two tribes, similar to many in the Old Testament, except that their wanderings brought them to the Americas, first in 2250 BC then in 600 BC. They came, Kon Tiki-like, across the Atlantic in barges.

The leader of that second wave of wetbacks was Lehi, a former Israelite. Two of his sons Laman and Lemuel had been cursed by God for their disobedience. They were on the run.

The descendants of Lemuel became the black races of North America; the Lamanites became the American Indians. To this day blacks cannot achieve full membership of the Mormon Church although Indians (now known with due political correctness as Native Americans) can. Some do.

In 34 AD, goes Mormon lore, Jesus Christ, following His crucifixion and resurrection, came down from Heaven to North America, where the blacks and Indians had settled among some whites whose origin is not explained. Christ instructed the whites, known as Nephites, in the sacraments of baptism and communion and introduced them to such articles of 'Christian' faith as the Sermon on the Mount.

In 385 AD, near the hill of Cumorah, nearly all the Nephites were killed in a battle with the Lamanites. Moroni, however, survived. He was, at that time, mortal, the son of a scribe named Mormon, who had been recording all these events on the golden tablets that were eventually revealed to Smith. How Moroni became an angel is, like much of Mormon doctrine, not entirely clear.

It is not the story attributed to the golden tablets that draws the wrath and disdain of other churches upon the Mormons but the rest of their distinctly 'un-Christian' theology. Mormons are ready to accept some of the Bible as Holy Writ. However, they insist that much of it was incorrectly translated – until they came along. The creed postulated by Joseph Smith and upheld by his celebrated, gun-slinging, much-married successor Brigham Young comes into direct conflict with several generally shared Christian beliefs.

To be technical, Mormons believe that God the Father and Adam are the same Personage. And that God *physically* fathered Jesus Christ with Mary – forget virgin birth. They believe that God the Father and Jesus Christ are *physical* beings but that the Holy Ghost, the third pillar of the Christian trinity, is not. As Smith, displaying his rustic impatience with such refinements of theology, wrote in another key Mormon document, *Doctrine Covenants*:

> The Father has a body of flesh and bones as tangible as man's; the Son also; but the Holy Ghost has not a body of flesh and bones but is a personage of Spirit. Were it not so the Holy Ghost could not dwell in us.

Quite.

For Mormons, salvation does not come, as mainstream Christian belief would have it, by the intercession of Christ who died for the sins of all mankind. They believe they must achieve it by atonement for sins, by good works and by personal observances. These accomplished, they – the menfolk, at any rate – will become gods themselves in the hereafter.

Mormon women do not do quite as well. If they have a husband they may be fortunate enough, through the unique ritual of 'Celestial Marriage', to share his salvation. A considerable step beyond ordinary, earthly marriage, this celestial version ensures that the wife, too, will survive into eternity as a 'goddess'. Thus, a Mormon girl has quite a lot at stake in a relationship.

Of the many curious things about the Mormon Church the most astonishing are the arrangements made for people who died before they were able to benefit from Joseph Smith's revelations. If they can be identified, their life and death documented, they too can be saved and will be united with the faithful throughout eternity. The living descendants of those unfortunates are encouraged by the church to rescue them by a process of posthumous and retroactive baptism in which the dead are represented by a living Mormon. Kirk Anderson's mother explained to a reporter that she had often played the part of such a substitute. 'Our belief is that it gives those dead people an opportunity they did not have in life to come into our church,' she said. 'It is a very moving experience.'

Those who are to be saved in this way, however, must be the *genuine* ancestors of someone living. It is not enough for God to know who these imperilled souls may be. There must be proof of their family tree to satisfy the Mormon bureaucracy. To this end, the Mormons have bored a huge complex of caves into the granite heart of the mountains overlooking the Great Salt Lake. Within these air conditioned lairs, safe from anything short of nuclear holocaust, millions of microfilmed dossiers hold birth, death and marriage records, parish registers, land deeds harvested from all over the world by indefatigable Mormon investigators. It was one of these collections in London that Joy found so helpful when she needed to borrow an identity.

The same preoccupation with the concrete and tangible lies behind the Mormon ordinances against smoking, drinking alcohol, tea or coffee – even, strictly speaking, innocuous stimulants such as Coca-Cola. The bodies of this life must last their owners through all eternity. They have to be looked after.

Then, of course, there is the article of faith that characterises Mormons in the minds of people with only a casual interest in them, the fascinating concept of polygamous marriage. That was about all that Jill Evans, a refugee from the valleys and the chapels of distant Wales, had heard about them before she set out for her first quick but revealing peek into Joy's past.

– 7 –

The idea that a man might have many wives was not one of Joseph Smith's original concepts. It came to him by the process that has remained central to the operation of the Church: Divine Revelation. The original Mormons left New York in 1831 for the state of Missouri where – according to a Revelation – they would be able to build a land of their own, a new Zion. Revelation or not, this large band of pushy settlers preaching their curious ways did not find a welcome among the Christian fundamentalists who had already spread through that territory.

In 1839 the pioneers took to the wagon trains once more; the opening sortie of a migration that became one of the most epic in the opening of the West. First they went to Illinois and negotiated with the government of the young state for a piece of its Hancock County, in which to build the city of Joseph Smith's dreams. They called it Nauvoo. In quite a short time the industry and organisation for which Mormons would become renowned, combined with their skill at recruitment, turned the site into the largest and most prosperous city for hundreds of miles. More than 11,000 settlers built some 2,000 homes there and began the construction of a temple that would cost a sum that only a few of them could grasp: one million dollars.

Nauvoo became virtually an independent nation within the United States. Smith, who had previously been content to be called The Prophet, began to be referred to as General, a fit title for the leader of so disciplined and devout a legion. It was in Nauvoo that Smith received the Revelation that bestowed divine sanction on multiple marriage, at least for eminences such as himself and his 'cabinet', grandly designated the Council of the Twelve Apostles.

The speedy growth of Nauvoo and tales that came out of the

place soon alarmed other citizens of Illinois. Trouble came to Zion. Renegade Saints accused their leaders of degeneracy and corruption. 'Gentiles' – as the Mormon faithful still refer to outsiders, even Jews – began to look into what was going on.

The first encounter soon occurred in a chain of savage clashes between Mormons and Gentiles that was to last for decades and leave a trail of bloodstains across half of the United States. It also gave the church its first martyrs. Smith and his brother, Nyrum, were arrested in the town of Carthage, Illinois, not far from Nauvoo. They were taken to the local jail where several followers voluntarily joined them. The governor of the state had guaranteed the Mormons protection against lynch mobs, but on June 27, 1884, the jail was stormed and the two Smiths shot to death

Brigham Young, the senior of the Twelve Apostles, a housepainter before he became one of Smith's early converts, emerged as a Yankee Moses. He marched the Saints and himself into American legend. (For those who prefer myths, the 1940 Hollywood version *Brigham Young*, starring Dean Jagger and Tyrone Power, is occasionally resurrected as a late-night movie.) He also endorsed the idea of more-the-merrier marriage wholeheartedly, showing a fine example by taking over five of the 27 widows that Smith left behind.

Brigham – as Mormons invariably call him – and his 'Avenging Angels', sharpshooting frontiersmen Saints, opened up a guerrilla war on the Gentiles. In return, vengeful Gentiles burned Mormon crops, desecrated the Temple, took brutal advantage of the plentiful wives. Western Illinois became a terror-ridden battlefield for two years before the state was able to expel the Saints, whom Brigham then led on a great westward trek through the Rockies in search of yet another Zion, battling Indians, terrible weather, and some of the most hostile terrain on the continent.

Even as the Saints struggled into the unknown, their ranks were being reinforced by converts shipped out by tireless missionaries in the Eastern states and even beyond the Atlantic Ocean. Spreading the Word and bringing in the souls had become part of the Mormon way of life but for the moment bodies were more important. The first human crop the Mormons set out to harvest was in Britain.

Brigham had sailed to Liverpool in 1840 in search of new blood. His eloquent promises of a heavenly kingdom with gilded thrones for the uplifted lured thousands of poor Britons away from the squalor of factories, the slavery of tenant farms. The first British convert was baptised in the River Ribble in Lancashire in 1837. By 1855 a third of all immigrants to the United States were newly enlisted Mormons.

In the summer of 1847, having come 1,100 miles from Nauvoo, much of it on foot, Brigham and his 147 pioneer companions reached the huge, desolate mountain-ringed plain in which lay America's own Dead Sea, the Great Salt Lake. On the map it was Mexican territory and Brigham believed they would be safe there from marauding Gentiles. Although the land was arid, the soil poisoned by the salt crystals that impregnated it, there were lakes in the mountains where the water was clear and sweet. 'This is the place,' he said, naming it Deseret, the scriptural word for a bee, and calling the local river the Jordan. He was 46 and had 17 wives.

Congress outlawed polygamy in 1862. The Utah Territory, yet to become one of the United States, took little notice up until the time of Brigham's death in 1877. It finally realised that Washington meant business when a Supreme Court decision in 1884 sent more than a thousand Saints to prison, ordered the deregistration of the Church as a business and federal marshals began to confiscate its property. Farming came to a standstill in whole sections. Crops went unharvested. Thousands of families were left fatherless while the marshals rounded-up fleeing Mormon husbands all over the range.

Congress, exasperated, warned that unless there was an end to polygamy, Utah would not be admitted to full statehood. Its goods would be barred from the trans-continental railroad that in 1869 had been linked with a golden spike at Odgen, the other city beside the Great Salt Lake. It would be ostracised within the America nation, its people shunned, its economy ruined.

47

The pennywise Saints pondered their options. And in 1890 Wilfred Woodruff, Joseph Smith's third successor, now known as the President of the Church, was blessed with a timely Revelation. Despite the 'everlasting covenant' by which the Prophet Smith had established plural marriage, the practice, it seemed, was now anathema to God. Henceforth it would mean excommunication and disgrace.

Utah became the 45th state in 1896, and the Church, broke and disorganised by its battles, turned to the resources the Saints still show so vividly: industry, tenacity, parsimony. And a willingness to do as they are told.

As the Saints recovered from their privations, as the desert began to bloom and as, tireless as ants, they built the Zion that Brigham had promised, the money began to roll in. The Church soon switched from the primitive collectivism that Brigham had preached to the vigorous capitalism on which the rest of the United States had begun to thrive. Tithing helped a lot. In the early days when Brigham tried to exact a tenth of every Mormon's income he had often got nothing. Nonetheless he died rich, scorned by sneering Gentiles as 'The Profit'.

There are four million Mormons throughout the world – 102,000 of them in Britain – and they were increasing at the rate of 200,000 a year. Each one of them must contribute ten percent of what he or she earns, before taxes, to the Church. The wealth this adds up to, and what happens to it, is as deeply veiled in mystery as the Saints' innermost rites.

There have, however, been astute estimates. In 1937 the Church's income was calculated at a million dollars a year, respectable enough in those Depression days. But in 1976, a series of articles by Associated Press reporters David Briscoe and Bill Beacham classified the Church among the fifty largest corporations in the United States. The investigators concluded that its combined income from tithes, and investments had reached about a billion dollars annually. At the rate of exchange Joyce Kinney got when she financed her visit to Britain, that would equal nearly £1.5 million a day.

No newspaper in Utah carried those AP stories on Mormon

money. Neither are they inclined to publish much about the many thousands of Saints who, to the huge embarrassment of the greater Church, persist in polygamy to this day. The renegades insist that they are following the unsullied beliefs of Smith and Brigham. They remind others that, Divine Revelation or not, Wilfred Woodruff himself did not give up his many wives until the federal government prosecuted him. These dissident Mormons are beyond the law. At least twenty-one of them have been killed one way or another, in the last few years. When Saints fall out among themselves their vengeance is often violent.

Joy had heard all these stories during her eager conversion to her new faith but not been deterred. Soon she would have stories of her own to tell.

Britain's national newspapers, which are headquartered in London, and the great provincial morning papers, have little enough time to get stories in print overnight and their various editions distributed throughout the British Isles. Evening papers, particularly the ones that serve Greater London, the *Evening Standard* and the *London Evening News* (which closed down in 1980), have even less. Their editorial staff begin work on the early editions long before daybreak. The first evening paper reporters are heading out on their assignments only an hour or so after the last sub-editor from the nationals is on the way home.

The pressure to get stories into the constantly revised editions of the *News* and the *Standard* before the button must be pushed to start the new print run breeds a special kind of newsman. The stand-up reporter. An evening newspaperman with only minutes to go to his deadline will pick up the telephone on the bank manager's desk before he even asks the first question about the hold-up. At the other end of the line his dictated copy will be snatched, sentence by sentence, from the copytaker's typewriter and put before a sub-editor who must instantly mark up the type in which it is to be set, write a headline and – if there is time – scan the text for errors and even rewrite it for maximum impact. Although the reporters rarely have a chance to polish a phrase or a 'lead', the best of them have mastered the knack of turning their notes – if they have any – into crisp, clear sentences so that the sub-editor will be less tempted to reshape the story.

The early editions of the evenings usually give late-rising national newspaper executives the first taste of the stories that are developing. On November 23, the first day of the committal hearing at the end of which the magistrates must decide whether there was a sufficiently strong case to send Joy and Keith for a full-scale trial at the Old Bailey, Mike Molloy and his deputy editor, Peter Thompson, a tow-haired, hard-nosed Australian, read them together in Molloy's office. Thanks to Joy's insistence that reporting restrictions be lifted, the long-awaited disclosure of the nub of the Mormon Case (as it had now been labelled) was right there where it belonged: on the front page of both evenings. The facts hardly needed dramatising. All the rumours the *Mirror* reporters had been bringing in stood suddenly transformed into authoritative print. Even if it did not develop further, the story – the oddest either Molloy or Thompson had come across in their tabloid lifetimes – would be the talk of Britain the following day. It would sell hundreds of thousands of newspapers.

Court reporting against the clock is among the most demanding of the stand-up jobs because reporters must stick to what has been disclosed in court and may paraphrase only with great care. The *News* 'splash' story under the joint by-line of Tony Frost and Paul Smith – aided perhaps by an anonymous sub – was a model of its kind, laconic and logical.

> A young Mormon missionary told today how an ex-beauty queen kidnapped him and then made love to him while he was chained to a bed in a lonely cottage.

A little long for a tabloid lead. But which word could possibly have been dropped?

> Kirk Anderson, 21, said the girl, Joy McKinney, and her friend, Keith May, tied down his arms and legs with leather straps, padlocks, chains and rope, so that he was spreadeagled.
>
> May then left the room while Miss McKinney tore off his blue silk pyjamas.

Then came Kirk's actual words, a choice quote:

> 'She grabbed my pyjamas from just around my neck and tore them from my body. The chains were tight and I could not move. She proceeded to have intercourse.
>
> 'I did not want it to happen. I was very upset.'

She proceeded to have intercourse? Having got its most 'grabbing' point across, the story could draw breath in order to get some formalities out of the way.

Mr Anderson was giving evidence to Epsom magistrates where Miss McKinney and May are accused of abducting him from the Mormon church in Banstead Road, Epsom, last September and with imprisoning him against his will.

Then it settled down to lay out these amazing disclosures.

Mr Neil Denison QC for the prosecution, said Miss McKinney had 'an all-consuming passion' for Mr Anderson. She had chased him thousands of miles across America and eventually to Britain.

Mr Anderson described how he had been kidnapped and taken to a cottage in Devon. The ransom for his release was to make Miss McKinney, aged 27, pregnant.

He said he met May, who was using the name Bob Bosler, at the church in Epsom by appointment on September 14.

'I felt him push something into my ribs, and he grabbed my shoulder.

'I was startled, and as I looked down I saw it was a gun. I was quite scared.

'He told me to come with him. I did not then know the gun was an imitation.

'He took me over to a car parked about 50 yards away. I got into the rear seat. Joy was in the front seat wearing a dark wig and she had another gun.

'I thought that was real, too.

'She said something like how did I think 8,000 miles of ocean was going to keep us apart or something to that effect.

'She got into the back seat with me about five minutes after we left the chapel. She told me to put my head down, and Bob told her to put a blanket over my head so I could not see where I was going.

'We were going at high speed and after a couple of hours I tried to push the blanket up a little bit. As I did so I saw a sign which said Yeovil.

'When I was allowed to remove the blanket I saw I was inside a garage and I was taken to a cottage adjoining it. I had no idea where I was.

'I was taken to the bedroom and allowed to sit while Joy cooked dinner. They explained that they had brought me to the cottage so we could sort out the things that had happened since I had known her.

'She told me she still loved me and wanted to marry me. She said I could be there for two or three months and she intended that we should just be together from that time on.

'I spent that night with Joy in the same room. Nothing of a physical nature took place – most of the night I was listening to her.'

Only much later could anyone imagine what an ordeal it must

have been to be compelled, helpless, to listen to Joy's self-righteous outpourings. The enthralling story continued:

> 'Bob placed a leather strap attached to a chain on my leg the next day and he attached the chain to the bed. It was about 10ft long so I could in fact move off the bed but not very far. He said he had to chain me for her protection.
>
> 'I had thought about escape but I really did not know where I was. I decided if I tried to cooperate gain their confidence I would be able to sort out a release.
>
> 'Joy told me there was to be a ransom. The ransom would be that I would have to give her another baby.
>
> 'That night she spent the night with me in bed. I kissed her and I held her in my arms. But there was nothing else. I was trying to cooperate.'
>
> He said he was forced to have sex with her on the third night. 'When she came into the room there was a fire in the fireplace and she put some music on. I recognised it because she had played it in the apartment two years earlier when we first had intercourse.
>
> 'She was wearing a negligee. She came to me as lay on the bed. I said I would like my back rubbed.'

Back rubs, it was later to be seen, were an important part of these people's erotic rituals.

> 'She proceeded to do that but I could tell she wanted to have intercourse again. I said I did not and she tried to convince me. She then left the room and returned a few minutes later with May.
>
> 'May was carrying a red flight bag and had chains, ropes and padlocks,' he said. May and McKinney used these to tie him down on his back to the four corners of the bed so he was spreadeagled. The chained love session then took place.
>
> Mr Denison asked: 'Although you didn't mentally want it to happen how could it physically have occurred ?'
>
> Mr Anderson replied: 'She had oral sex.'

Ordinarily Molloy and Thompson would have relished this barely credible story. They would be gloating over the impact it would make on readers once it was projected in the *Mirror*'s powerful style, with some of the asides explained and exploited. What, for example, did the reference to 'another' baby mean? But that morning they moodily folded up the evening papers and poured themselves a drink. Molloy and Thompson were the only members of the editorial staff on duty.

The smouldering dispute that stopped the paper from coming out at the time of Joy's first appearance had flared into an ugly confrontation. The management had suspended publication in London and drawn up dismissal notices for the entire London staff. It was a major tragedy. Out at Epsom, a small army of rival newsmen were getting the first real inkling of what Joy was about to do for their industry but there would be no *Mirror* that day to lap up the precious manna of the Mormon Case, apart from the Northern editions of 1.5 million or so – only about 30 per cent of the total circulation – produced by a separate staff and printing plant in Manchester.

As Kirk's hair-raising account of the brief affair and its outlandish consequences unreeled Joy and Keith sat in the dock holding hands like young lovers – which they were, after a fashion. He stroked her cheek. She squeezed his hand. If he wanted to take out a pencil to make a note he had to pry her fingers away from his.

Whenever Joy turned against the light her bosom was silhouetted in all its improbable magnificence. A police witness had confided to a reporter that when the couple had first been stopped at the roadblock one of the coppers took Keith aside and demanded to know, 'Are they real?' In the courthouse corridor Joy turned this way and that to make sure everyone could appreciate the profile. They *were* real, she assured the newsmen. 'All mine.' *And,* she managed to confide in a whisper, she never had to bother with a bra. Next day the great white wedge of her smile blazed across acres of newsprint.

– 9 –

The *Mirror*'s northern editor, Mike Taylor, was delighted to be able to show London how a big story should be handled. Union restrictions prevented a Manchester reporter being sent down from the North into an area that would have been covered by the London newsdesk, save for the stoppage. Taylor had to rely on copy from the Press Association, a newsagency owned jointly by the major papers, which distributed its reports by teleprinter.

Manchester gave Joy and Kirk matchless *Mirror* treatment. On page one the high points of the evidence were emblazoned. Pages two and three were turned into a 'fake spread,' presented as a single hard-hitting unit, as though they had been the centre-spread of the paper.

Across the top of that linked space a bold black rule centred the 'strap', a line of smallish type:

Round the world chase ended in 'bizarre bondage' for a young missionary.

Then came two lines of heavy capitals to carry the main message of the headlines:

KIDNAP BLONDE SHACKLED ME FOR SEX

Dovetailed into the lines of large type was a big picture of Kirk that the Mormons had innocently handed out. His jaw was square, his teeth were white and his gaze level. His hair was cut short, modishly trimmed into a widow's peak combed down over his forehead.

A subsidiary 'deck' of headlines was inspired by a letter that had been introduced into evidence on Joy's behalf and could thus, under court rules, be published:

Mormons tried to brand our child as a 'son of Satan'

There were pictures of the cottage and of the notorious bed. Column upon column of type laced with 'crossheads' for easier digestion ran to a length three times as great as the average *Mirror* story.

No reader would want to miss a single word of this. The versions of the story that had been thrown together hastily in the evening papers had provided little more than an outline of what had gone on in court. Television could do even less, merely offer basic details read out over shots of the participants going in and out of court.

This was a classic newspaper event of a kind not seen from one year's end to another.

In their efforts to shape thousands of words of copy to size, Taylor's sub-editors were considerably helped by the concise and masterly presentation of the case against Joy made by prosecutor Denison. 'This is a most unusual case,' Denison told the magistrates – in case they were wondering why their courtroom was packed.

Continuing, he obliged the press with an adjective the reporters could not have bettered. 'Firstly, because the facts can be described only as *bizarre*. Secondly, most of the facts cannot really be in dispute at all. What is in dispute is the interpretation.

'It seems that this young woman is consumed by two passions. The first is an obsessive hatred of the Mormon Church. The second is an excessive love or desire for the young man Kirk Anderson. The combination of these two obsessions culminated in these offences.'

Denison introduced the fact that Joy and Kirk had sex soon after they first met in Utah two years earlier. 'Who was the seducer and who was the seduced is not important,' he said. 'What is important is that the Mormon Church forbids sexual intercourse before marriage.'

Denison explained that Kirk had felt guilty about what had happened and gone to his bishop for advice. He later told Joy the affair was over. 'But she would not agree.'

That, of course, was putting it mildly.

Denison sketched out the lengths to which Joy had gone to

track Kirk down so far from home and Taylor told his subs to let it run and run.

> She persisted in trying to see Anderson. So much so that he was compelled to move to California, then to Oregon where he lived under an assumed name.

> When the time came for Anderson to do special missionary work he asked to be sent to Britain, rather than California, where he was originally bound, to avoid her.

> But she would not give up. In September 1976 Mr Anderson went to East Grinstead, then Reading, and finally to Epsom, where he lived in Milton Gardens.

> 'On February 14 this year Miss McKinney telephoned from California to a Mr Mann, who is employed by a firm of private detectives called the Finlay Bureau of Investigation, asking him to track down Mr Anderson.

> A week later she sent the detective a letter, enclosing £120.

A thoughtful court clerk had photocopied the letter for reporters. When more of her correspondence came to light later these instructions to the private eye could be seen as vintage Joy...

> This may be one of the most unique cases you have ever handled. Kirk is running away, using the cloak of religion to hide what he has done. You can never imagine how horrible they treated me when I became pregnant by Kirk who was then my fiancée.

> The Mormons put us up before our congregation and scorned us and told Kirk to break our engagement because I had given him my virginity and was not worthy of him.

> Kirk listened to their wild stories that I was 'from Satan' and our innocent baby was 'a child of Satan' born of lust of the flesh – a 'bastard'.

> They punished Kirk by shearing off his beautiful long hair in a ridiculous crewcut above his ears. They told him he would have to go through a period of repentance and sent him off on a mission to get him away from me and the baby.

> Poor Kirk was born and raised in Utah so he has never known anything but Mormonism. He is suffering so much guilt because of them. I, however, have been stronger than Kirk. I was able to see through Mormon lies and false doctrine.

> Although Kirk took my virtue, got me with child, and did me wrong, I still love him and want to marry him. There's nothing in the world I would not do to make that man happy. In order to do this I must find him first.

Joy signed the letter Beth Palmquist and added, 'Now – go get 'em.'

Palmquist...? The reporters noted yet another aka.

Denison explained how the detective had traced Kirk to Reading and then turned to its consequences. On August 5 Joy and Keith arrived at Heathrow Airport carrying false passports in the name of Kathie Vaughn Bare and Paul Van Deusen. Yet another aka was used to rent the cottage: Mr and Mrs Layton. Honeymooners.

On August 19, Keith (Bosler on that day) introduced himself to Kirk for the first time, expressing interest in joining the Mormon Church. Denison summed things up for the magistrates. 'There seems little, if any, doubt that Anderson was tied to the bed. Anderson says he did not want to have sexual intercourse. He says he was stimulated by McKinney and that she was the active partner.

'She says he was shackled to the bed but the chains were merely instruments to be used for what she referred to as bondage sex. She says Anderson was a totally willing partner.' The reporters took careful note of that. It was obviously to be Joy's defence.

So far the press had had eyes only for Joy. But now Kirk took the witness stand. Reporters sized up the young Mormon as he began to fill in the details of his first fateful encounter with Joy back in Utah.

He hardly seemed the kind of chap to inspire such desperate passion in a woman. He was bulky and shambling, easily 17 or 18 stone (236-252 lbs), with huge hands and feet; a bovine milk-fed look. He walked with a flat-footed lurch.

He wore aviator glasses. The hair that Joy mourned was carefully trimmed into the modish cut all young Mormons seemed to fancy: sort of Country and Western.

Later, when Joy was free on bail and she was asked what had attracted her to Kirk, her eyes clouded with remembered rapture. She breathed, 'He was the sweetest-smelling, cleanest man *Ah* ever knew. He used to shower and wash himself two, three times a day. Every little hair was perfectly clean.

'And his skin. *Ah* just loved to smell his skin...'

Just as disarmingly, Joy amplified the story Kirk was to tell in court of having tried to make love with her in the living room of her house in Provo while her parents, who were visiting, were asleep in the bedroom. 'Daddy came out and caught us in the middle,' she recalled with a demure flutter of lashes. 'He spluttered and said he was just going to get a glass of water. But poor Kirk. ..' Joy's raised index finger described an eloquent downward curl for her fascinated listeners.

'He just went like *thaaat...*'

When Denison asked Kirk if he had found Joy beautiful when they first met, the Mormon was less than gallant. That first encounter had occurred when they had driven up, separately, to an ice-cream parlour in the main street of Provo. Joy must have been hard to miss – blonde, dressed with her usual flamboyance, and seated in a persimmon-coloured Chevrolet Corvette, America's flashiest sports car.

Said Kirk: 'It was the car I noticed first.'

Kirk told the court that he and Joy had met only twice when she told him she loved him and wanted to marry him before he was due to depart on his two-year stretch as a missionary. Later, after he had sought advice from his bishop about breaking the rule of chastity, he told her he would not be seeing her any more.

'She did not accept that position'.

That seemed to be putting it mildly if what he subsequently related was true.

'A few days later I was riding home on a motorcycle,' he explained, 'because the tyres of my car had been slashed. McKinney pulled up behind me in a car and tried to stop me. I drove off the road and managed to ride home where she made towards me screaming and kicking. She was very upset that I wouldn't go to a party.'

Then came his first-hand version of Joy's alleged assault on him the cottage and its immediate aftermath. He intrigued his audience by explaining that Joy had ripped off not only his pyjamas but his 'garment'. He was referring to the Temple Garment, a tight one-piece item, like an old-fashioned swimsuit, worn by pious Mormon men and women to help restrain them from sins of the flesh.

Garments are embroidered with sacred symbols and have a slit over the heart to symbolise the fate that could await a traitor to the Church. Kirk told of burning his once it had been defiled. He said that after being forced to have sex he had been extremely depressed and upset. 'I lost my temper and at one point I picked her up and threw her across the bed. She said she was going get what she wanted whether I wanted to or not. She said she might keep me there for another month or so until she missed her period. I promised to marry her just so I could get back to Epsom.'

Stuart Elgrod, Joy's solicitor, was eager to get a few things clear about events at the cottage. Exactly how many times did Kirk have intercourse with his client on that fateful Friday night? Three times, Kirk told him. But it had been against his will because 'I knew I would be chained up again if I didn't'.

Elgrod: 'I am suggesting that at no stage were you ever tied up in that cottage, except for the purposes of sex games.'

'No, no – that's wrong,' Kirk protested. He said that on the Thursday night Keith chained him to the bed by his legs 'for Joy's protection'. Keith had left the house and he was alone with Joy for 24 hours. The chain was long enough, he explained, to let him reach the kitchen and toilet.

Elgrod: 'The next day you were joking about it – it [the chain]came off with a can opener. You were completely unfettered.'

Kirk: 'I was bolted in.'

Elgrod: 'You didn't even try to escape?'

Kirk: 'No – I knew I was going back soon anyway.'

Elgrod put it to Kirk that after he had been brought back to London he and Joy had gone to the American Express office in Haymarket. There was no gun, the solicitor reminded him, no Keith. Other people were present and yet he had not tried to escape.

'Because I was going to Epsom,' Kirk replied. In fact he Joyce and Keith had also gone for a stroll in Trafalgar Square together and, longing for a hamburger – poor exiles – had lunched at the Hard Rock Cafe in Piccadilly. Still Kirk had not tried to get away.

Elgrod read out part of a letter that lawyers in Provo acting for Joy had sent Kirk two years earlier, asserting that she had had a positive pregnancy test. The letter said she would not have an abortion, or have the child adopted. She wanted to get married and if Kirk did not comply he would be taken to court.

Kirk told Elrod he did not believe Joy had ever conceived. 'She told me three days after we had intercourse that she was positively pregnant,' he said. 'That is one reason.' Later, Joy had told him – as she was ready to tell anyone – that she had miscarried.

But all this was ranging too far afield from the crucial matter of abduction and the magistrates needed to be reminded of the main issue. Mr Denison brought the proceedings into focus by asking Kirk the critical question: had he gone to the cottage willingly? 'No.'

Joy and Keith were sent back to their separate jails, remanded in custody for another week.

Bondage, Blonde, Bishops, Shackles, Sex, Satan, Pregnancy, Magic Knickers, Did-he-or-didn't-he? Could she or couldn't she? God bless America!

For his sermon to the *Mirror*'s Northern circulation department, whose reps were preparing to descend on every newsagent in the area and urge them to pile the copies high, Taylor chose his text from Joy's letter to the Finlay Bureau. 'Now – go get 'em.'

In London Molloy and Thompson brooded. The atmosphere in which negotiations over the stoppage were being conducted was becoming more embittered by the hour. The *Mirror* would be lucky if it was back in business before the magistrates decided whether Joy and Keith had a case to answer.

Sulking at home, temporarily on the opposite side of the dreadful paperless no-man's-land of the dispute, news editor Shillum read the accounts in the opposition papers, his usual healthy scepticism mingled with envy. He is a portly man whose thick spectacles give him a benevolent air that is as misleading as Joy's big brown eyes.

One of a news editor's incidental talents is the ability to sniff out any weaknesses in a story before he or his newspaper is made to look foolish. Shillum was less interested in the banquet of goodies that the Queen v. Joyce McKinney was providing to the hungry multitudes of the media than in what was yet to reach the table. He was concentrating, as folk-wisdom counselled, less upon the sugary doughnut than upon the hole. He could see several holes in the story so far.

Why had Kirk not been chained up until the THIRD day he had spent at the cottage ?

Why had Keith left Kirk and Joy ALONE there for 24 hours?

Why had Kirk lost his temper only AFTER, as he had put it, 'She proceeded to have intercourse'?

And what about Joy and Keith? Were *they* lovers? Why had Keith helped her ensnare Kirk? The pair of them had mounted an elaborate and fairly costly operation. Fake passports, cars, the cottage… Where had the money come from?

– 10 –

Salt Lake City is tethered to the town of Provo by 40 miles of Interstate Highway 15 as a great ship lies to a sheet-anchor. The anchor is not the town of Provo itself, a flattish sprawl of supermarkets, fast-food joints and ticky-tacky housing framed, far beyond its rightful desserts, by some of the most spectacular peaks in the Americas, the Wasatch Mountains: it is Brigham Young University.

'The World Is Our Campus,' says the slogan emblazoned on the gates of BYU: 'Go Forth To Serve.' In their hundreds, virginal young men like Kirk Anderson go forth at the age of 19 or so to scour the world for new Mormons as, in the days of the draft, other young Americans would troop off to military service. Nearly all male graduates of BYU put in their two and a half dedicated years, whether among the Lamanites in Wyoming just across the border or the heathen around Epsom. Two thousand of them combed Britain daily.

A wry favourite ballad on the juke boxes of the cheerily teetotal hangouts around Provo was called *BYU Boy Missionary*. In Centre Street, shops boasted, 'Everything for the Missionary'. A storefront window displayed 'The Missionary Suit' in indestructible Swedish man-made fibre, 'Two Pants and Vest in Navy, Brown and Green.' There was also a portable snakebite kit. Serpent-bites, thought Evans, playfully. She knew her Bible.

Because Jill Evans arrived in Provo before Kirk had poured out his rueful story in court she, like Buckland over in Avery County, had no idea of exactly what was supposed to have happened to him. She had been briefed, though, about the intriguing claim in Joy's Bible messages that the *Mirror* had not been able to get into print: *He Had Sex With Me For Four Days*. So she knew broadly what was needed: discover the basis of this

63

curious romance. Little of what she might unearth could legally be published until Joy had been tried or the charges dismissed, but once either conclusion had been reached every nugget Evans could mine in Utah would be regarded as the purest gold – if there was ever again going to be a *Mirror* in which it could glitter.

By the end of her first day Evans and other wandering British correspondents, with whom she compared a few cautious notes when their paths converged, were equally baffled and frustrated. A source would be friendly, open – even flattered to be interviewed – when first approached by telephone. By the time the reporter arrived on their doorstep an hour later the same person would be evasive, hesitant: useless. A woman who had been cheerfully talkative in the phone call would be represented by a silent, forbidding husband. It did not take the reporters long to realise that their enquiries had fired up a sensitive and efficient network. They christened the phenomenon the Mormon Doubleback.

Only about 30 percent of the 1,235,000 population of Utah was Mormon in 1978. But the Gentile contingent of Brigham Young University, which had 25,000 students, was so small that it could perch on the spires of the Temple with footroom to spare. BYU is the largest educational establishment operated by a church anywhere on earth. It produced doctors and engineers, lawyers and journalists, footballers and drum-majorettes just like any American university. But Harvard it was not. Nor Yale nor Columbia nor Berkley, with their free-swinging 1970s ways, co-educational dormitories, campus taverns and political frolics.

A BYU student could not smoke nor drink intoxicating liquor. There was nowhere, anyway, where they could go to drink it. The state of Utah was not dry. Nor wet; just grudgingly damp. State-owned stores sold liquor by the bottle and supermarkets beer by the can. But there were no convivial pubs or gathering places where students could let off steam.

Male students were not allowed to grow long hair or moustaches. Young women could wear anything so long as it was decent and concealing. Some went in for high-bodied,

64

ankle-length dresses that pleasantly accentuated the Western flavour of the place. If a student wanted to keep a cow to supply him with milk, the university would accommodate it.

Accommodation for the students themselves was controlled – to the immense profit of local landlords – by the university's Office of Standards. The standards were not those that applied to the condition of the houses and apartments in question that were often decrepit. The term meant the strictures of the church against smoking, drinking and even the *possibility* of fornication that were mercilessly enforced by the landlords and property managers, many of whom were Mormon bishops, the sergeant-majors of the Sainthood. Unmarried men and women students were not even permitted to live in the same building unless arrangements for their segregation were of a suitably secure order. Visitors of the opposite sex had to be received publicly and visibly – no closed doors – and at limited hours.

Restrictions such as those are far from novel to the young Saints who arrive from all over the world each year to enrol at BYU. All Mormon communities submit to a tight rein. In the subdivision of Orem, where Kirk and Joy both lived, the 40,000 residents were ninety-one per cent Mormon. They were divided into 'missions', a certain number of which comprised 'branches' that expanded into 'wards', 39 of those in the case of the Oremites. The wards, each under the direction of a bishop, were the key unit of the fine-mesh net in which the Church enfolded its people. So many wards constituted a 'stake', whose president was a significant rung higher on the executive ladder than a bishop.

Within this close-knit and highly efficient system, which is replicated in Mormon colonies the world over, supervision is benevolent but intense. A bishop, or some other eagle-eyed keeper of the faith, will visit every home in the ward at least three times a year. He sees every member of his flock at services each Sunday and at other times when they frequent the chapels. The chapels are often attached to social centres used for basketball, one favourite Mormon pastime, and dancing which, despite the general puritanism of the Church, is another. Dances are an especially busy time for a bishop and his henchmen. The fierce strictures against premarital indulgence make sex a weighty preoccupation for Mormon youth. Any mixed gathering of BYU students fairly reeked with suppressed lust.

Mormons oppose abortion and what they call 'population control'. Marriages take place early. Families are expected to be large. And to play together as well as pray together. Monday nights are family nights, the traditional time for whole clans to gather under one roof. There might be a reading from the Book of Mormon or a discussion of someone's troubles. The spirit of mutual dependence, bred in the frontier days, still helps bind the Saints together. They look after their own.

Every good Mormon provider is expected to keep a year's supply of food in the home. For general emergencies, and for the genuinely needy, each ward has a Bishops' Storehouse, packed with products packaged under the church's own label, Deseret Brand – 'the brand that money can't buy'. The price of the goodies in the Storehouses is the same as for any other benefits that this exclusive, self-protective society has to offer. Good conduct. Keep the faith.

The cost of straying from the path of righteousness, as Kirk had done, was high. News of wavering observances or nonconformity in the matter of morals travelled fast, usually in the direction of the bishop. A lapse in any direction would bring him down like a bill collector. Only perhaps in some totalitarian regime where each street block in a city had its party cadre or commissar might a community come under closer or more constant surveillance.

A faithful, obedient and industrious Mormon need lack nothing in life – education, companionship, employment, security – as long as the church remained satisfied that he deserved it. If not, he must look after himself, on earth as well as in the hereafter. Backsliders who fell for the temptations of cigarettes and whisky got the contemptuous label of 'Jack Mormon' slapped on them. Even for a cup of coffee – let alone for the wild, wild likes of a Joy McKinney.

Instinctively, Jill Evans followed the moves that Joy herself had made when she hit town four years earlier. She too headed for the Osmonds. In 1973 the clan that *Life* magazine once referred to wonderingly as 'a plague of wholesomeness', were probably more famous in Britain back then than they had yet become in much of the United States. Their concerts and television appearances won them three records in the Top Ten, something not even the Beatles at the height of their greatness had achieved. A whole generation of British pubescents squealed themselves silly over little Jimmy bawling out his incongruous claim to be a 'long-haired lover from Liverpool'.

To Mormons everywhere the Osmonds represented the glittering pinnacle of a growing aristocracy within the Church of show business and sporting celebrities. The King Family were Mormons. So were golfers Billy Casper and Johnny Miller. In Provo, where they returned to be among their own after achieving global fame, the Osmonds were royalty. Not only Alan, Wayne, Merrill, Jay, Donny, Jimmy and Marie, the performers. But Virl and Tommy, the eldest brothers, both deaf from childhood but with sound business heads. And, of course, Mother Olive, who also marketed tape recordings of *The Story of Joseph Smith*.

Joy arrived from Avery County, aglow with the rapture of her new-found Sainthood, serenely convinced that the acclaim she had longed for all her life must soon be hers. The Osmonds were the most glamorous thing she had ever seen. There was no doubt in her mind from the beginning that she belonged at their side.

– 11 –

Accompanied by the huge, shaggy sheepdog Millie, who went with her everywhere, Joy enrolled at the BYU School of Theatre and Cinematic Arts. That school, together with the Communication department which taught TV and journalism, prepared Mormons for careers in entertainment and the media. 'Don't call me Joyce,' she would repeat to the men she met – she rarely wasted time talking to women. 'My name is Joy. Like in *Joy To The World.* You know ... the hymn'.

Just outside the university was a huge complex of student apartments called The Riviera. It was owned by the Osmonds and many of them lived there. Joy moved in, antennae alert. But the Osmonds, like the rest of Provo, were not quite ready for Joy. She was just too much for her well-scrubbed co-religionists, particularly the home-grown ones. She flaunted herself in outfits that were gaudy, gauzy and, by the standards of folk who always buttoned up carefully and shunned adornment, downright outrageous. Her hair was the blondest east of Hollywood Boulevard. The twin peaks she projected ahead were as hard to overlook as the snow-capped Wasatch. When she took off her robe at the Riviera's swimming pool in the hope of attracting admiring Osmond eyes, a hush would fall and many a silent prayer float heavenward.

By the time Evans got to the huge compound in Orem that housed the family's multi-million dollar record and publishing business Olive Osmond had nothing more to say about Joy. When the story first broke Olive had been willing to talk extensively, if noncommittally. All she would say now was that the lady had been 'somewhat of a problem'.

The Doubleback was also in force at Evans's next stop, the arrestingly modest little house from which Kirk Anderson had been catapulted to notoriety. Barbara Anderson was a huge, broad woman, easily apparent in Kirk, had Evans ever seen a picture of him. But she had nothing to say about her son by now and not much about Joy either.

Because Kirk had not yet come out with his startling allegations against Joy, Evans was feeling her way through unknown territory. She had few wiles to use on someone like Barbara, apart from womanly sympathy, which did not get her far. 'We were so anxious when we heard of his ordeal,' said Barbara, predictably enough. 'And so relieved when he was released. He has telephoned us to say that he is all right and will be staying on for another year in Britain to complete his Mission.'

Evans did learn something about the sacrifices that families like the Andersons were expected to make in order to fulfill that Mission, the dream that warms the hearts of every good Mormon mother and son. Kirk had two younger brothers and a sister. His father was a caretaker at the local school. Household income would have been barely above the poverty line. Yet, even after paying their tithe to the church, the Andersons had been so determined to honour Kirk's ambition that they scraped together his fare to London. They still had to find the £100 or so that it cost each month to keep him there.

In Barbara Anderson the faith ran deep. A correspondent from the *Sunday Mirror*, Gordon Gregor, who also interviewed her at this time, was mesmerised by her account of acting as a stand-in for people from the vast ancestral archives whom the Mormons set out to baptise posthumously. 'You cannot help but wonder what the person looked like, what they did in life,' said Barbara, rapturously. 'Where they lived, if they were happy. I have felt the presence of a person I was standing in for. Others say they have actually seen a recognisable face or figure materialise.'

Even though their newspapers belonged to the same group, Gregor and Evans did not regard themselves as being on the same side in their efforts to scrape together what they could about Kirk's background. Some of the sharper rivalry in Fleet Street is between daily newspapers and their Sunday coyunterparts. Sunday journalists are always in search of something that is either exclusive or will far outweigh whatever has been written about a particular story during the week. They are haunted by the fear that whatever they get their hands on will not stay out of the dailies until the one day out of seven that they have a chance to publish. Daily journalists become similarly unnerved as the weekend closes in on a story that is running hot, strong and fast. Should the climax be snatched away by the Sundays, their week would be ruined. Gregor, a seasoned and persistent Scot, knew he had to get one step ahead of the other correspondents knocking on doors throughout Provo and Orem and stay there. But like them, he had no idea where the trail was leading. Or, indeed, where it began.

Evans eventually realised that the only way the Osmonds were going to talk was through their public-relations man, Ron Clark. Reporters and PRs are natural enemies, mutually mistrustful. But she had to get *something* on Joy's claim to have been engaged to Wayne, the soft-spoken brother who was usually first-on-the-left on stage. Olive Osmond had been too polite to sneer but Clark did it for her. 'It wasn't Wayne in particular. She hung around a lot, wanting to go out with any one of the boys. She certainly made her presence felt in great abundance.'

Evans waited for more. 'There are countless girls who want to be near the Osmonds,' Clark continued, 'and fantasise about their friendships with them as more than just fans. The Osmonds are a friendly family and have always taken time to talk to fans who wait after concerts or outside their front door.'

Evans realised that she was being invited to see Joy as a mere groupie, that hardly seemed to fit even with the little that was apparent at that point about her feats in Britain. Also, Joy had been 23 at the time, years older than the average Osmond fan.

Really? said Evans, her eyes wide, flattering Clark with unswerving attention. Do go on. 'But Joyce McKinney,' said the PR, sternly, 'overstepped the privileges of a fan who was shown friendship.'

So Wayne had seen Joy as a friend? 'Joyce McKinney always wanted to be close by whenever and wherever possible,' said Clark. He came up with a term Evans rather liked: 'She became very possessive of a light friendship.'

Clark had clearly found such girlish folly distasteful. 'Now we've had to put up notices to ward off trespassers and loiterers. It's distressing because the Osmonds are such a lovely family who wouldn't want to hurt anyone.'

Oh, well, thought Evans, possible story leads running through her mind. A light friendship is better than no friendship at all. Although if Joy had compelled the Osmonds to put up the barricades she must have been something more than a lightweight nuisance.

Evans was reluctant to take the unsupported word of an Osmond publicist that Joy's 'abundant presence' had been no more than a slight bother. She called on the Chief of the Provo Police Department, Swen Nielson – who turned out also to be a bishop. As it happened, his ward was the one in which several of the Osmonds worshipped. Sure enough, Joy had once approached Nielson in church looking not for Wayne but for Merrill. 'Afterwards, Merrill told me she had been bothering his family,' said Nielson.'But I never had any formal complaints as a policeman.'

Later on, Gregor managed to get past the guards and warning notices for a tour of the huge studio complex on which the Osmonds had spent more than £1m – but only on condition that he did not ask about Joy. He found Donny Osmond joking with lighting technicians about the girl he was taking to dinner that night at Robert Redford's ski resort, Sundance Lodge. A few of the cracks his audience came up with verged on the *risqué* for good Mormons... 'opening an account... making a deposit'. But Donny knew when to stop. 'Hey, guys we'd better cut it out now,' he said. 'Enough. That's my date you're talking about.'

Donny showed Gregor around the auditorium where at taping time the seats are filled with adoring BYU students and outside; the family planned to build housing developments where there were orchards at present. The streets would be named for one or another Osmond. Wayne Way, Donny Drive, Alan Avenue.

'The interest in this project is fantastic,' said Donny, enthusing about the studio. 'Lots of people want to use it. Even major Hollywood productions. 'The President is coming to dedicate it, you know.' Donny was not talking about Jimmy Carter. To a Mormon, the President meant 82-year-old Spencer Kimball, First President of the Church. If anyone deserved the honour of a presidential visit it was the Osmonds. The annual tithe from their income was more than a million dollars.

The *Daily Mirror* picture desk had been begging Evans to dig up some photographs from Joy's days as a beauty contestant. Even though Joy had not yet boasted about her title attempts in court, word had leaked that she was once a contender of some sort. The president of the Provo Chamber of Commerce, Gordon Bullock, who organised the annual Miss Provo Contest, was no help with pictures. But he did come up with the first portrayal of Joy as a loser. A bad one.

In 1973 Joy had come second in the contest. In 1974 she had been third. 'She never actually won the title she coveted,' said Bullock. 'And she indicated her displeasure of this in very strong terms. When I went up to congratulate her she said very abruptly that she had no desire to be anything but the queen.'

Bullock still found the matter puzzling. 'Most girls are delighted just to be in the finals,' he said. 'It was quite a shock when she didn't smile, just stared right through me and made that comment. I didn't know what to say. It was so embarrassing and such a bad influence on the other girls that we had to stop Joyce entering a third time. Normally we go all out to encourage girls to enter and it was a precedent for her to be refused. But her behaviour had been so emotional and neurotic that we felt it was bad for the other candidates.'

Then Bullock provided Evans with an assessment of Joy that was as revealing as a reporter could want. 'She was a girl who set her sights on something and would go to extreme lengths to reach her objective. She was the same in the man-seeking department. She would get infatuated with certain fellows who did not share her intensity of feelings. After one or two dates she would pursue the relationship, even though the fellow wanted to terminate it. I suppose this part of her nature is a sign of her motives related to her activities with Elder Anderson.' Spot on, Brother Bullock.

Evans could see that trying to keep Joy out of a beauty contest must have been like trying to stifle the squeals at an Osmond concert. After that first failure in the local contest she had picked herself up and headed for the big time. Or what, from little old Provo, must have looked like it to Joy.

– 12 –

Dorothy Mitchell was a worldly 60-year-old who ran the Barbizon School of Modelling from a gingerbread mansion in Salt Lake City. She was not a Mormon. She smoked, although she did not take it up until was 40. She drove a satiny black Jaguar XK120 with wire wheels; when the chrome needed touching up she forked out a thousand dollars and thought it well-spent.

Joy went to Dorothy because she held the concession for the Miss World contest and several similar events in Utah and the surrounding states. Joy desperately wanted a crack at that title.

'I mainly get country girls,' said Dorothy, elegant in a beige pants suit, surrounded by the trophies and mementos her protégés had collected. 'Raw material. *Very* raw. Joy was a little better educated than the usual run of them. And a little older. She was very well proportioned in those days. And very single-minded. She sat right there and said: I'm going to be famous one day.'

The Miss Wyoming candidacy was vacant. Joy got together some sponsors to finance her trip to New York, where the finals were to be held to decide which girl would go the climactic event in London as Miss USA. She satisfied a few minor formalities and the privilege of representing a state that she had never even visited was hers.

The preliminary heats for the rival Miss Universe contest were already over for that year. Joy flung herself into those, too, Dorothy recalled. There had been different sections. Costume. Swimsuit. Evening Dress. Personality. With true actor's ingenuity, Joy carried off the Universe award in Costume by decking herself out as a seagull. The gull is a favourite symbol of Utah because a flock of them saved the crops of the early

Mormons settlers from a plague of locusts. The birds arrived just in time to eat the insects.

Apart from that partial triumph, Joy's efforts were wasted. She was eliminated. 'She tried and tried and tried,' Dorothy recalled. 'She was the sweetest young woman. Until something went wrong. And then – watch out!'

Dorothy's manager, Kent, had also seen the hopefuls come and go through the beauty pageant hoops for years, 'The trouble with Joy,' he said, 'was that she thought she was a goddess already.'

In Binghampton, New York, where the Miss World contestants appeared on television with Bob Hope, Joy had some conditions to lay down. Much as she wanted the crown, she said, she would not abandon her religious principles to win it. She told compere Dick Clark that if she were to win the title it must be understood that as a good Mormon she would not be able to carry out any duties on a Sunday. 'I would never even be able to go out and eat on Sunday,' she said. 'Never do anything that could make work for others on the Sabbath Day.'

As it happened, that was the year Marjorie Wallace became Miss USA, went on to win the Miss World title and then was stripped of it because of her brazen sex life. Pious and provincial Joy must have thought she was on the right track to be strict, although Sabbath observance was among the many principles she was later to abandon in her overheated pursuit of Kirk.

Joy took out her failure to win the title on Alfred Petrocelli, the US franchiser of the Miss World pageant, who begged Dorothy Mitchell, 'Please don't send me any more like that!'

'She was always late for everything,' Petrocelli remembered. 'Always took hours to get ready.' That was a failing that everyone that everyone who knew Joy would remark on.

'She was real mad when she lost,' said Petrocelli. 'The day after the judging she called the police and complained that her room-mate had stolen $300 from her. Then a little bit after they arrived and made a big scene she found the money. It looked to me as if she was just trying to be the centre of attention to make up for not winning.'

In Dorothy Mitchell's experience, girl contestants were invariably thrilled to the core by simply participating in the wild world of big beauty pageants, whether they won or lost. 'When they came back home they would be on the telephone as soon they got off the plane,' she said. 'Even while they were still at the airport.'

Not Joy. Dorothy never heard a word from her then or later. 'I've got something to remember her by, though,' said Dorothy. She produced a promissory note for $250 dollars, the entrance fee for the contest that Joy had not been able to come up with.

The second address at which Joy had lived in Provo was University Villa, an apartment complex managed by Harold and Helen Smith. Kindly people. Good Mormons. 'She came down here after they'd had enough of her up at The Riviera,' said Mrs Smith. 'Normally we wouldn't have taken the dog. But she told us that Millie was the only friend she had in the whole world.'

No boyfriends? 'Only a couple of young men came around. And they soon stopped coming. She seemed to scare them off.

'We made lots of special exceptions for her,' Mrs Smith went on. 'We let her take an apartment by herself rather than share. It was expensive for one student alone but she said she could just call up home whenever she needed money.' Joy could and did. David McKinney could deny his daughter nothing.

Accustomed to the austere life-style of the average BYU student, the Smiths had been stunned at the mountain of luggage Joy brought with her. 'I never saw so many clothes,' said Helen. 'Such piles of make-up. Such a collection of wigs and hair-pieces. When she was going somewhere it would take her hours to get ready. She would get very angry if you saw her as she really was – before she was ready to make an entrance. Still, we knew she was studying to be an actress. She would always tell us: One day I'm going to be famous.'

Even the Tourism Director of Utah at the time Evans was working at her interviews admitted that outsiders often found the people of his state backward and unfriendly. It certainly began to seem that way to Joy. She complained that people would not take her and her ambitions seriously.

The Smiths finally got fed up with Joy because of her temper tantrums. Most people who spent any time in Joy's company had been treated to one of those. 'She was really high-strung', said Harold Smith. 'She would just flip her cork for the slightest thing. And she would have arguments with the other students. We suggested to her that she would happier in a place where she would feel more on her own.'

That was the little semi-detached house in north Provo where, a couple of years later, on a waterbed she thoughtfully installed in the living room, she and Kirk would play out the defloration scene she was to describe in court. The house was owned by Dottie Majers, to whom Joy would sometimes turn for an audience for her histrionic suicide threats.

Recalled Dottie, a no-nonsense woman, 'She'd say to me, "If people don't stop treating me like I don't exist. I'm going to kill myself." I'd tell her if you're going to do it, make good and sure you do it outside. Don't mess the house up.'

Joy became an even greater source of fascination to the little suburban community when her father, trying to buoy up her morale, bought her the persimmon Corvette that was to entrance Kirk. The colour was shattering. And with Old English Millie seated beside her and her blonde hair streaming Joy was a more memorable sight than ever.

During this time Joy had a nominal speech-training job at BYU. She was acting in student plays and getting on with work for her doctorate, if not very earnestly. One of her few friends had been a high-school student, Marilyn Clark, then 15. Marilyn's mother had been agreeable to an interview when Jill Evans telephoned. She sounded extremely promising. Joy, she said, had been a very bad influence on her daughter. But, at the time arranged, the Mormon Doubleback had kicked in and Evans was greeted on the doorstep by Mr Clark – Hoover – a BYU professor of French. The family had decided *not* to say anything, after all.

Professor Clark, a scholarly figure in bifocals, his shirt pocket sprouting ballpoints, was too polite to refuse to answer questions altogether. Evans managed to elicit a fascinating snippet. His daughter – one of four – had followed Joy to Los Angeles.

'She fell under Joy's influence very strongly,' said Clark, sadly. 'Joy always sought the company of people younger than herself.' This did seem to be the case. Kirk was five years younger; Keith three years younger.

'Joyce McKinney could convince people that she was very different from her reality,' said the professor. Which was? 'Well... she took a course with me. She was very disorganised. I couldn't see how anyone as helpless about her private life could ever attain a doctorate.'

On the subject of Kirk, Professor Clark went along with the Mormon party line. 'She made his life miserable. He didn't want anything do with her. But she wouldn't accept it.'

Evans looked over the notes she had gathered from all her sources and reckoned she must be ahead of her rivals, whose movements she had been able to keep up with through their contacts with the local Provo newspaper, the *Daily Herald*. The reporter handling the story there was Pat Christian, a friendly, James Cagney-ish Mormon from San Francisco. Visiting reporters traditionally trade information with their local counterparts and almost every one of them who came to town turned him for help eventually. It did not take long for the British correspondents knocking on doors in Provo to realise that Pat was telling them a good deal less than they were telling him. Wondering about the Church's intelligence system, they began to keep their distance.

For all the progress she had made, Evans still had more questions than answers. Kirk, she could now picture as a rather simple, unworldly young man for whom Joy would have been more than a match. She was puzzled that anyone who had set her cap at an Osmond would consider a baby-faced trombone player an adequate replacement, although there seemed little doubt that was what Joy had done. Even the waitress at the

Holiday Inn where Evans was staying, Dorothy White, knew all about it. She had gone to the same church as Joy and Kirk.

'She made life miserable for that young missionary', said Dorothy. 'She even told him she was pregnant to stop him going away.' Did she now? Thank you, Dorothy. London was yet to hear of this matter from Joy herself.

As for Joy, Evans saw that she clearly had an insatiable hunger for the spotlight, an exaggerated view of her own appeal, a fondness for getting her own way and a carefree attitude to other people's money. Although, thought Evans, a lot of men she knew would describe half the women in the world that way.

Evans was not sure what to make of Professor Clark's story of his daughter falling under Joy's influence. Also, it was hard to see someone with the kind of grinding determination that Joy had displayed in the rest of her endeavours attempting suicide simply because the Osmond Family had snubbed her. If that *was* all that had happened. And if Joy *had* tried to kill herself. Evans made one more trip to the *Daily Herald* for a poke through the files.

Wayne Osmond, she found, had announced his engagement in November 1974. By that time Joy had been telling everyone for months that he and she were an item. Evans telephoned the Utah Valley Hospital, the medical complex that serves Provo and Orem. Sure enough, Joy had been something of a regular there, although they would not say why. She had first been admitted in October 1973, after her frustrating Miss World fiasco. She had been admitted again on 25 August 1974, after her second failure in the Miss Provo contest. Again on November 12, after Wayne Osmond had announced his engagement to one Kathlyn White. And again on December 19, six days after the wedding.

The ease with which such details could be obtained in America was something that British reporters never ceased to wonder at – and be grateful for. Evans could see that Joy might have sought hospital attention every time she suffered a nasty shock to the ego. The Osmond marriage must have been a particularly cruel blow, to judge by the clippings. The bride, twenty-three-old

Kathlyn, had been that year's Miss Utah, an honour Joy would have envied deeply. All the more, since in order to marry her knight of bubblegum rock, Kathlyn had to give up being a Miss. She tossed the precious title away as blithely as her bridal bouquet.

One persistent rumour Evans was never able to confirm. Several people told her they had heard that after the crisis of Joy's relationship with Kirk she had checked into the Timpanogos Community Mental Health Center in Provo. This was troubling. On the one hand there was ample material for a tasty 'backgrounder': a portrait of a wacky American who would seem extremely exotic to *Mirror* readers, when the legal proceedings were over and it could be published. On the other hand, there were strong suggestions that Joy might be a deeply disturbed young woman.

Anyway, Evans could spend no more time in Utah. This was not the only story in the western states that she was expected to cover. Also, once back at her Los Angeles base she would be able to plough up Keith May's past in California, which might help plug other gaps in the saga. That, of course, was before Joy made her final court appearance in Epsom and won her place in the history of our times with the most spellbinding outburst ever recorded in a British courtroom.

– 13 –

When that great day came, the *Mirror* was back in the hands of its readers all over Britain, if only just. The dispute between journalists and management had turned into a 10-day cliff-hanger that ended only 48 hours before the preliminary hearings against Joy and Keith reached their final phase. The millions of copies of the *Mirror* that had never been printed, never been sold, had become engraved in Mike Molloy's mind like lists of the dead on a war memorial. A story like Joy's that was just hitting its stride was worth hundreds of thousands in circulation every day to the papers able to run it.

On November 29, the moribund *Mirror* executives had watched sullenly from the sidelines while the proceedings got under way with Prosecutor Denison reading out the statements Joy and Keith were alleged to have made to the police after their arrest three months earlier. Once more the Epsom court was jammed, reporters competing for seats with housewives who crowded into the public benches with their shopping bags.

Joy insisted from the start that Kirk had been a willing party to the diverting events at the cottage. The police noted that when she heard that Kirk in his statement said he had only been 'pretending' to cooperate with her she became hysterical. 'You mean he said I was making everything up?' she asked. 'He says he doesn't love me? Let me see this person I've given three years of my life to.'

Whoever had transcribed Joy's tape-recorded statements had taken pains over it. Despite Denison's deliberately deadpan delivery, her authentic voice came through. Her anguish, genuine or assumed, was unmistakable. 'He telephoned my parents and said he was marrying me,' she had told her interrogator. 'I can't believe this. It never occurred to me he would lie. The number of times he said he loved me...' Back in Provo they might have recognised Joy's best drama-school style.

The reporters nodded sagely. The old, old story of a woman spurned. Her father, sitting in the court with her mother, whispered loyally, 'Scoundrel!'

Joy told the police how she had come to be disillusioned with her adopted faith. She recalled her first days of rooming at The Riviera. 'I don't smoke or drink. I was put in with three girls who were drunkards. One was a bishop's daughter. I was left out and unwanted. They called me Little Miss Perfect.'

She explained how hard it had been to find a good man in Provo. 'I went out with missionary after missionary. One guy tried to rape me. They weren't anywhere near the standard I expected.'

Her version of the affair with Kirk was a good deal more lyrical than the one he had given the police. She could have been dictating a story for *True Confessions* when she recalled the scene at the ice-cream shop. 'Kirk pulled in beside me and my heart did sort of flip-flops. He was really putting the makes on me. You know, "What's your name? What's your car?" Usual first-date things.'

By Joy's account, Kirk he had not really needed the chat-up lines. Joy, however, was only part of the appeal for him. 'I'll never forgot the first quiver when I looked at him,' said Joy. 'He smiled a slow smile and said: "Why don't you let me drive that Corvette?"'

'I was quite smitten with him so I said, Sure! That night I felt more in love than I'd ever been in my whole life. He liked all the things I did: music, theatre, animals, babies. And he was so quiet and reserved.

'He didn't try to grab at me or ask me to have intercourse. I appreciated that. And he appreciated me. He was looking for a girl like me, and I was really happy.

'He asked me to go steady and I said, "We're too old for that." Then he said, "Let's get married." I couldn't think I was so lucky...' A couple of the Epsom ladies dabbed their eyes.

Joy sat demurely in the dock as her enthralled audience hung on Denison's recital. 'So, since he and I wanted a family real bad, we decided on a marriage in May. Because Kirk would have turned 20 in May. He said he didn't want my friends to tease me over getting married to a teenager.' Joy was 25 at that time and, in the youthful BYU community, keenly conscious of it.

There was an additional consideration. 'OK, I didn't want to wait till May, because things were getting really heavy. We didn't have intercourse. He just teased me and kissed me until I was out of my mind. I didn't want to do anything wrong because I had saved myself so long.'

Joy explained that her parents were appalled at the thought of a Mormon son-in-law. 'When I had joined the Mormon Church my parents got down on their knees and begged me not to do it.' As Gentiles, the McKinneys would not even have been allowed to attend a wedding in the Temple. 'There was a great deal of pressure from my family not to marry Kirk,' Joy said. 'I was too blind to see it.'

During a recess, while the reporters were filing their stories from whatever telephones they could find in shops and houses around the courthouse, a slightly built young American with corrugated hair moulded to his head confronted Kirk. Earlier, he had been talking to Joy's mother and father; none of the reporters had paid him particular attention. Now, he shocked people standing near by saying to the young missionary in a loud and disgusted tone: 'You son-of -a-bitch!'

Shocked, Kirk shrank back amid his Mormon minders. The stranger walked away. Later, a detective who had seen what happened approached him quietly, asked him to repeat what he had said and explain why he had said it. As a matter of interest, said the detective, just who was he?

Of all the accounts from Epsom that had made Molloy squirm with envy in his silent office was one in the *Daily Mail*, written by John Edwards, a former *Mirror* star. The *Mail* had got hold of a picture of Joy posing proud and wide-eyed in a swimsuit and her Miss Wyoming sash. In the piece accompanying it, Edwards, a deft encapsulator of atmosphere, marvelled at the array of exhibits on display that included the gear Joy had used to lash her lover down. 'On a table in the back of the court,' he wrote. 'There were chains and shackles, coils of mooring rope and four-inch galvanised bolts. It looked like the corner of a ship chandler's.'

Privately, Edwards, not a leg man when it came to women, shared in the general fascination with Joy's cantilevered bosom. Whenever she swung it against the light he found himself sighing gently and neglecting his shorthand notes. But he kept his edged gaze on Kirk and his poker-faced co-religionists as Denison moved on to Joy's account of the troubles her new-found lover had run into with his Bishop. He did not think much of what he saw. 'The few Mormons in court,' he wrote, 'watched like embarrassed statues. One of them had tennis shoes on; another had dandruff in his eyebrows.'

As Denison, not always successful at keeping his tone neutral, moved on to Joy's highly coloured version of the first time that she and Kirk had made love, her mother paled and seemed ready to faint. Joy had gone into lavish detail about surrendering her virginity on the water-bed she had installed in the living room of the little house in Provo in anticipation, she explained to the police, of the marriage she had believed imminent.

When, three years later, Joy set out to restage her defloration in the Devon cottage she could not run to a waterbed. But so powerful was her urge for verisimilitude that, in addition to the same music and food she and Kirk had enjoyed on that fateful night, Kirk had been lashed down upon the very same quilt that had cushioned their capers in Provo. Joy had shipped it over.

That fateful night in Provo, Joy related, Kirk had said something about the waterbed like 'Let's try it out' and 'Put on something sexy for me'. Then, she rattled on, 'Knowing he'd had an upsetting time with his bishop, I wanted to make the day better for him – like any wife would do for any husband. I put on a sexy nightgown. I took a shower and he was under the cover nude. So we can distinguish who made the advances.'

She got across a plug for the credentials she was always ready to recite. 'I'm 38-24-36, so I don't have to beg for boys' services. I was Miss Wyoming in the USA pageant, so I didn't have to seduce boys. Any rate, he pulled me into bed.'

This occasion – perhaps Kirk's defloration as well – was the only time the couple actually had sex until they were together again at the cottage in Devon, two years later. Then, recalled Joy, he said, 'Joy, my precious little virgin, I am so glad you waited for me.' Denison had warmed to his task. There were perceptible nuances as he switched between voices.

Joy had said: 'I told him we couldn't have intercourse that day. We had to have our white wedding in a church. It was very important to me. But I didn't reckon how it would feel to be in a big king-size bed with your betrothed. So Kirk started teasing me and then he got on top of me and started to penetrate me. I said, "Hey, babe, we gotta wait." I was pretty aroused.'

After this little tussle, Joy said, she had begun to fear she might be pregnant. Kirk told her not to worry. They would be getting married anyway. According to her, he added: 'I want to see your blonde-haired babies running around the house.'

If this affectionate declaration had been intended to make them feel less guilty, the effect was short-lived. As Joy told it, a disconcerting change came over her satiated lover. 'He started raving about what the church was going to do to him, he started acting strange, like he was going into a trance. He got strangely quiet... his eyes got glazey... he said he had to go see the bishop.'

The following day, Kirk made an abrupt departure. He appeared to have realised that on the eve of setting out on his mission he had committed a sin that could cost him everything he might gain as a dutiful Mormon. 'He went to this bishop,' said Joy. 'And in the typical way of the Mormon Church, he was completely ripped apart. He was told I was not worthy of him. He should break off our engagement.'

Joy knew something had happened. 'I was getting panicky. If I called at his house his mother answered and wouldn't let me speak. I couldn't understand how he could talk about marriage... It never occurred to me that the man didn't love me until I read his statement.'

In later episodes of the enthralling serial that was emerging from the police statements Joy told her interrogators that she had not passively accepted the role of the woman wronged. Putting her enquiring mind to work on the problems she thought Kirk might be having, she turned to authorities such as Dr Alex Comfort, author of *The Joy of Sex*.

Joy devoured sex books. She had taken a speed-reading course and claimed to be able to get through a paperback in thirty minutes, or so. One of her favourites was *Total Womanhood*, a best-seller by Marabel Morgan – a Mormon. Ms Morgan quoted the Scriptures extensively in support of her advice to American housewives about how to pamper their husbands sexually. She suggested they should greet the old man at the front door wearing a shortie nightie and high heels. Or just a frilly apron and some scent.

Another book Joy had been reading right up until the moment that she pounced on Kirk was *The Sensuous Woman*, whose author, identified only as 'J', gushed: 'Oral sex is, for most people who will give it a real try, delicious. It is part of the Sensuous Woman's bag of pleasures and has the added advantage, if you're a snob, of being a status style of lovemaking. (It's the preferred way with many movie stars, artists, titled Europeans and jet-setters).' It was to be quite a while before the extent to which Joy might have taken this advice to heart became apparent.

At that stage Joy just told the attentive coppers who had taken all this down how she had come to understand that feelings of guilt prevented some men from enjoying sex. They might be cured, she learned, by participating in games of sexual bondage in which the woman was the aggressor. 'So, when I came over to England I was looking for a real romantic cottage where we could have a honeymoon and I decided to play some of those bondage games with him,' she concluded her statement, winningly. 'We had such a fun time – just like old times!'

But the old times, noted Alan Shillum from his enforced seat on the sidelines, had taken place quite a long while back. Joy had hardly given three years of her life to Kirk – as she claimed. They appeared to have been together for only a few weeks.

Where had she been between that time in Orem three years ago and her arrival in Britain? Where had a good Christian young woman – as Joy insisted she had remained, even though she was no longer a Mormon – learned tricks like those she had applied to Kirk in the Devon hideaway? Not entirely, Shillum would bet, from reading *The Sensuous Woman*.

The statements Joy had given the police did not mention a further source of inspiration that she was most willing to discuss with reporters once she had been freed on bail. Her favourite work of fiction was *The Other Side of Midnight* by Sidney Sheldon. Its heroine, Noelle Page – 'famous for her beauty and notorious for her sexual appetites', according to the paperback blurb – had been seduced and abandoned by a dashing young man. Years later, Noelle sought him out to avenge herself and became the star of a dramatic trial. Joy told everyone she 'identified' with Noelle Page.

The magistrates adjourned their hearing for another week. Joy and Keith went back to jail until December 6. By then, to the immense relief of Molloy and his frustrated team, the *Mirror* would get a proper chance at the story at last. The dispute that had frozen production was settled and the London presses began to turn again.

When next the pair appeared, Garth Gibbs was assigned to write the 'colour' story, as opposed to an account of the proceedings: to describe the ambiance of the court, the audience reaction, talk to Joy's parents. Reporting the evidence was taken over by an older colleague, John Jackson, a master of the craft.

Even though this occasion was likely to be the climax of the long drawn-out proceedings that Joy had set off, media expectations had simmered down. All the juicy details anyone had a right to hope for had surely been poured out in Joy's nakedly explicit statements that had been read in the court the previous week.

The most that could be expected were formalities: a decision by the magistrates on whether the prosecution had shown there was sufficient evidence for the two Americans to be tried on a charge of kidnapping and whether Joy and Keith would be granted bail.

Joy's solicitor, Stuart Elgrod, had been tireless in his efforts to get her freed. He had made four applications before the magistrates for bail and one to a High Court judge. All had been refused. The police continued to insist that Joy was likely to abscond or try to harm herself. The general opinion among the reporters was that the occasion was unlikely to produce anything as good as the stories that Joy's statements had produced. How very much Britain had yet to learn about the blonde hillbilly sensation who had burst bra-less into its heart.

– 14 –

John Jackson looks as though he belongs in a courtroom, not necessarily on the press bench. He has a wise, high-coloured, patrician face that would go well with a barrister's horsehair wig and gown. He was delighted to be back at work. But he had difficulty finding somewhere to sit in the jammed courtroom.

Low expectations or not, the realisation that this might be Joy's final appearance in the lengthy committal proceedings drew reporters not just from London but from as far away as Birmingham, 120 miles distant. Word had spread even more widely among the good ladies of Royal Epsom of the fine free entertainment that was to be had. Row upon row of them filled the public gallery, murmuring with subdued excitement as they awaited the entrance of the magistrates, two men and a woman, who had to decide the immediate fate of the strange creatures who had been brought before them. Dozens more spectators queued for the first seat to be vacated.

The rummage-sale array of exhibits that had intrigued Edwards still covered the same table. As before, Joy and Keith were nestled side by side in the gloomy dock dominating the centre of the room. She wore a pink dress. Her hair was lacquered into up-swept wings and decorated with a white bow. On a table at which Stuart Elgrod and other lawyers sat lay a folder. From the dock Joy could read the lettering on its cover, *The Queen v. Joyce McKinney*. 'What have I done to the Queen?' she whispered to the prison officer standing by her. A defiant little joke. 'It's just the way it's put,' he whispered back, consolingly.

Joy had brought a folder of her own into court. It lay beside her on the seat of the dock. On the cover was written, in her spiky, rambling hand, *The Greatest Love Story Ever Told*. The pages it contained told Joy's own version of the story that was making her infamous. The version that mattered much more to her was taking shape in the screenplay she had also begun to write in Holloway, wanted eventually to direct and, of course, star in. In Joy's cosmic docu-drama today's events at Epsom were merely a run-through.

Some routine police evidence had to be gone over for the prosecution, the fine details of Keith having purchased the chains that had been used to bind Kirk. Kirk himself was not in court but his Mormon entourage sat stolidly in place. When Elgrod rose to speak, they were the subject of his first remarks. There was no question of the Mormon Church being on trial, he said. But, with a glance toward the Mormons present, he told the magistrates that they were entitled to take into account the Mormon way of life. 'It is quite clear from what we know that any further relapse by Mr Anderson would result immediately in his being sent home and excommunicated,' Elgrod said, implying that that was the real reason Kirk had complained about the sexual frolicking with Joy that had led to this prosecution.

Robert Marshall Andrews, defending Keith May, also drew attention to the Mormons. It was clear, he said, that his client believed he was not carrying out a kidnap but a rescue from an 'oppressive and tyrannical organisation'.

Into the courtroom drifted the raised voices of three women demonstrators who were being thrown out of the building. 'Women get raped every day,' they shouted. 'What is all the fuss about?' One of them, Susie Gabor, told Garth Gibbs that they had come there in response to an appeal from Joy. Joy was hardly a women's libber. But she wanted all the support she could get.

Elgrod embarked on a renewed submission for dismissal of the charges against his client. It was a well-polished and colourful exposition of the story so far. He mounted a scornful attack on Kirk's account of his supposed ordeal, emphasising that pleasure rather than pain had been lavished upon the young missionary and pointing out the many opportunities he had failed to take to escape. 'You could not commit a cat on this evidence,' said Elrod, with fine contempt. 'Let alone this young lady.'

As for the young lady's motives, Elgrod quoted the *Song of Solomon*. 'Many waters cannot quench love, neither can the floods drown it.' He then confounded the reporters by giving a twist to a passage of Shakespeare. 'Methinks the Mormon doth protest too much,' he declaimed. The press bench squabbled under its breath about which play the quotation had been adapted from. Jackson got it right: Hamlet.

But these bold efforts were all but forgotten when, during the lunch recess, it became known that Joy had decided to exercise her right to speak for herself. As strongly as he possibly could, Elgrod had advised against this. He might as well have dug in his dictionary of quotations for Thackeray's vision of King Canute holding up his hand against the sea and crying 'Back, thou foaming brine!'

Every playwright, every actor – even every BYU drama student – knows you can never go wrong with a trial scene. Joy rose in the dock, took one deep breath and launched the opening lines of one that her audience in the hushed court would not forget in a hurry.

'During the past three months,' she said, projecting like a trouper, 'I have been trying to get word to the outside world. But my letters from prison have been stopped and I have not been allowed to speak to reporters. I was in great fear that Kirk Anderson's lies and fabrications would be printed before the public learned the truth. Unfortunately this has happened.'

This was hardly the case. Both she and Keith had sent out many letters from their respective prisons (he was in Brixton, a far nastier place than Holloway). Joy had often spoken to reporters throughout the committal proceedings, although they were not able to publish what she had said; even opened delicate negotiations with some of them. She had soon cottoned on to the idea that in the right circumstances she could be worth a lot of money. She understood that the exclusive account of Joy's life and wondrous times would be a sure-fire circulation booster.

The campaign that Joy was shaping around her protestations of innocence had begun in those letters. The most recent one, for the *Avery Journal,* was waiting to be posted:

> As you may know, in England (in our case it seems, anyway) it is 'Guilty until proven innocent', not 'Innocent until proven guilty' as in our own United States.
>
> I was arrested, kept away 72 hours with a light shining in my eyes, forced to make a statement without a lawyer present and thrown (without trial) into a horrid English dungeon for three months with drug addicts, lesbians, prostitutes and murderers.

Joy was also receiving letters by the bagful, some from folks back in Avery County who had not seen her for five years. Hundreds of admirers all over the world, whose imagination had been stimulated by what they read in the papers, sent her good wishes.

Looking boldly around the courtroom, Joy showed that she knew how to keep the reporters alert, getting across a firm hint of sex before their attention could stray. 'I have been played up as a very wicked and perverted woman. It is not true. *He* is the one who has to be tied up.' Kirk, of course. A demure hint of playfulness trickled in to her voice as she added, 'I prefer to do things the normal way.'

Then she switched into the autobiography she seemed compelled to recite at every opportunity. 'I would like to tell you a little bit about my background and my life…'

The degrees were trotted out. The beauty contests. Her conversion to Mormonism. Every credential down to her Intelligence Quotient at the age of nine. ('Nine points above that of genius – I am not saying this just to toot my own horn.')

Joy was speaking fast, reading from the closely scrawled pages, fourteen of them, from the folder she had brought to court. Leafing through copies of the script handed up to them by Elgrod, the magistrates began to stir uneasily. The delighted media realised they had front-row seats at a virtuoso performance.

The reporters struggled to keep up with Joy's rattling delivery. Most wrote shorthand but they were not generally called on to get anything down at this length and pace. Nearly all of them had trouble with her breathy, dragged-out Southern-mountain accent. Television reporter Michael Brunson, recently back from a couple of years in Washington, provided whispered translations.

At last Joy paused. Drank water from a paper cup. She braced herself, raising the prow of her bosom defiantly. Edwards, bent on seeing that *Daily Mail* readers got their money's worth, knew he should look back at the courtroom, give the spectators' reactions a once-over. But he could not tear his eyes away from those breasts.

Joy turned to her traumatic disillusionment at BYU. The roommates who drank and had pictures of nude boys on the walls. '*Mah* goal,' she announced primly, 'was to find a decent clean-living Mormon boy to marry in the Mormon Temple and raise a big family with. *Ah* was searching for a boy who could read the Bible with me. The missionaries, whom I expected to be spiritual enough to be prospective husbands, were *wolves*.'

The Epsom housewives stirred sympathetically at this evocative term. Joy was encouraged. 'For a person who had been raised in a very Christian, warm, loving environment, it was like cold water being thrown on me. I didn't expect this at all. I was in a state of cultural shock. I prayed for a very special boy who would come into my life... and that is where Kirk comes in.'

She described the meeting with Kirk, much as both of them had related it to the police. Since making her first statement she had taken note of Kirk's crack about noticing the Corvette before he noticed her and got in a tart riposte for the record. 'I would like to say he did not propose marriage to the car – he proposed marriage to me.'

Now that at last she had a chance to speak her own piece there was plenty more that Joy intended to get off her spectacular chest. 'From then on we were together constantly,' she said, settling back into her narrative. 'We even had our children named. They were to be called Gabriel Kirk and Joshua Kyle. 'I said: "Honey, are you sure you can support me?" And he said: "Honey, I would work five jobs to support you".'

Reporters have a highly developed ear for authentic dialogue. This was a woman who had never forgotten as much as a cough that a suitor might have uttered in her presence. The press bench began to think it might actually be getting the real stuff – as rare in a courtroom as a fit of the giggles.

'To a woman this means something,' Joy read on, relentlessly. 'These are pretty heavy promises. He even promised to give me' – and her voice chimed out the quotation marks – "a rock so big my hand would sag".'

Scene after scene from the story she had waited so long to tell came tumbling out in no particular order. 'Kirk tries to say I tempted him. He told Epsom police I was wearing a skin-tight leopard skin jumpsuit. I had on blue jeans with a puffy-sleeved top – which has about as much sex-appeal as a potato sack.'

The reporters frowned. When was this? At the cottage she had worn a shortie nightdress, no? Was she referring to the first seduction, back in Provo? But earlier she said she had just come out of the shower. Never mind. Joy just wanted everyone to understand her sense of propriety. 'Any physical desire I felt was an indirect result of the real spiritual and mental love I had for him. A love he encouraged.'

And her sense of perspective. 'Believe me, after fighting guys off for 24 years, I wouldn't just give myself to a man unless he'd made some pretty heavy promises and marriage plans.'

Of sacrifice. 'I cannot say I ever got any pleasure out of sexual relations with Kirk. I was too busy trying to satisfy him.'

She even managed to squeeze divine sanction into the tumultuous narrative. When she and Kirk had made love for the first time, she said, 'It was the most special commitment in my life. It had made me his wife in God's eyes.' But, she went on resentfully, 'To him it was a quick thrill. Something we call a *casual* – something for him to cover up to his bishop and his mother.'

An edge crept into Joy's voice when she spoke of Kirk's mother. 'This isn't the first time he's accused me of raping him,' she said to the magistrates, confidingly 'He told the same story in Utah. A friend of his told me that he said to his mother: "Mom, she did everything. I just lay there. I didn't have anything to do with it".'

She sounded a note of outrage. 'Kirk's mother and his bishop told him I was bad for him and the baby was created from lust of the flesh.'

A note of despair. 'I tried very hard to be accepted by them but they were very cold to me. I was ostracised by the Church. If I walked on one side of the street they would walk on the other.' The reporters assumed she meant the Mormons.

Fear. 'My car was battered with a crowbar. I began receiving crazy phone calls in the middle of the night. Things like "Your baby's gonna die" – or I was going to die. The whole thing culminated when I was assaulted by two men who kicked me in the stomach. This, plus the stress of rejection, caused me to lose my baby.'

After this shocking – but never to be substantiated – reference, Joy thought it time to introduce some humour. She told of encountering Kirk and his mother in the street while she had been pregnant. He called out to her, 'Fuck you!'

'If you'll excuse my French,' said Joy, blushing up at the magistrates. 'I told him: "That is what you did, dear, and that is why we are in this mess".'

Accusing Kirk of sheltering behind his mother's skirts she said, 'He was like a scared little boy. Peeping out from behind her. I said, "Kirk, grow up, you son of a gun!" and he shouted, "Don't call my sweet mother names!" '

In less than an hour, Joy ran the theatrical gamut from high drama to comedy to bathos. All that could now be certain, as she rattled on, faster and faster, darting glances at the magistrates and reporters to gauge the reception she was getting, was that soon she would *craaaahh*. The tears began to flow, cued by the word 'baby'.

'I believe the spirit of Kirk's child is still living as much as you or me,' she said. 'And I believe I can still mother him one day.'

Spoken like a true Mormon bride.

– 15 –

The reporters were utterly engrossed. People simply did not behave in English courts like this self-possessed pink-blonde stranger determined to bare the most intimate details of her life. On the rare occasions someone does decide to say a few words on their own behalf from a witness box or dock it is usually a brief, halting and confused mumble. Only judges and barristers are expected to be eloquent – and they rarely come up to expectations.

Jackson flexed his cramped fingers and, spurred on by the page one by-line he knew must be his that night, scribbled as fast as he could. Joy began to tell of the overpowering love she felt for Kirk and what her efforts to put it into action had cost her – 'my entire savings, $17,000', that she had helpfully converted into £9,000. 'If I did not have faith in his love for me I could not have flown half-way round the world with my wedding band and my trousseau in my suitcase to see him. I loved him so much that if anybody had tried to shoot him I would have stepped in front of him and stopped the bullet.'

Accomplished professional actresses might have envied the skill with which Joy took the courtroom audience under her sway. The lawyers turned around from their table to stare up at her. Elgrod forgot his misgivings and smiled encouragement. A little earlier the magistrates who, ruffling through their copies of her statement, had interrupted testily to ask what page she was on fell silent, pressed back in their chairs.

Soon, anyway, Joy soared away from the script she had written. In a brilliant flash of improvisation she delivered the proclamation that was to endear her to the nation. 'I loved Kirk so much,' she said, 'that I would have skied down Mount Everest in the nude with a carnation up my nose.'

A shudder of delight shook the press bench. But the reporters had no time to savour the gift Joy so blithely flung them. She surged on, recalling Kirk's words when, at phoney gunpoint, Keith had brought him to her in the car at Ewell. 'Hi, pint-size,' she claimed he had said. 'Are you going to fight the whole Mormon army?' She gave a contemptuous toss of blonde hair. 'Kirk knew the guns were fakes and they had stage blanks in,' she said. 'I did not know they were illegal. I bought them in a souvenir store.'

Finally, she got around to the main issue. 'We made love several times at the cottage,' she said. 'If he didn't like it why didn't he just walk up to the people next door and say: "Excuse me, there's a girl in the cottage next door. She's kidnapped me. She's there cooking my favourite meals and baking me chocolate cake, giving me a better back-rub than my mother and making love with me"? Why didn't he do that? Because nobody would have believed him. They'd think he was a fool.'

Here was the diverting subject of back rubs that had arisen in earlier evidence. Kirk had admitted asking Joy to give him one at the onset of her alleged assault on him at the cottage. At the time Elgrod had swooped on this as suggesting that Joy was right; that Kirk had been enjoying himself. No, no, he had protested. There had been nothing sexual in his mind. His mother used often to rub his back.

Joyce turned up the scorn. 'A woman raping a man?' she sneered. 'Him eighteen stone and me eight stone?' Once again, for the court's convenience, she converted 250 lb and 112 lbs into measures that would be more easily grasped in England. 'Come on! Who's kidding whom?'

She gave her version of Kirk's reactions as she straddled him on the cottage bed. 'His claim that he was unwilling makes me laugh.' If he was so unwilling, she wanted to know, 'Then why was he lying there grinning like a monkey? Why was he moving his hips with me?'

Inhibition seemed to have gone overboard. 'I said, "Honey, does that feel good? Do you like it like this?" And he goes "Phew-HOT".'

Then she wondered if she might have been too frank. 'Sure it embarrasses me telling things like this. But it has to be told.'

Tears started again, this time petulant. 'His mother can rub his back from now on,' she said. 'I don't want any more to do with him.'

But self-confidence soon returned. She wanted the court to have the benefit of her scholarly research – as it was then assumed to be.

'At this point,' she said, with all the poise of a lecturer, 'I think I should explain sexual bondage and Kirk's sexual hang-ups. Kirk was raised by a very dominant mother. He has a lot of guilt about sex because his mother has overprotected him all his life. When we make love he has to have the lights out and wash up afterwards. He believes truly that sex is dirty...

'Kirk has to be tied up to have an orgasm. I co-operated because I loved him and wanted to help him. Sexual bondage turns him on because he doesn't have to feel guilty. The thought of being powerless before a woman seems to excite him. I didn't have to give him oral sex... I did it at his request because he likes it.'

Seemingly in wonder at the recollection, she paused. 'It was just amazing... he kept going and going..' Then she remembered where she was and what all this had led her to. 'He's had all kinds of temper tantrums after sex,' she reflected. 'I guess putting me in prison is an extension of these tantrums. He wants sex but hates me afterwards.'

She anticipated some questions that might have sprung up in the minds of her audience. 'Why didn't I marry someone who didn't have kinky hang-ups?' she asked, rhetorically. 'I loved him and wanted to help him. Many men go to prostitutes because their wives can't or won't satisfy their desires and fantasies. I wanted to keep him happy in bed. I wanted to satisfy and pleasure him. I'm a very old-fashioned girl. I believe a man should be pampered.'

Eventually, she seemed to acknowledge that she was, after all, defending herself against serious allegations and emphasised that she had only done what Kirk had wanted. She had devised a game in which 'you gradually remove the ropes until you can make love normally'...

'I would like to point out that I acted out a sexual bondage scene that was directed by Mr Anderson. I was supposed to be the aggressor, to play-act a part of a beautiful woman who had him in her love prison.

'He laid down on the bed for me and let me tie him up. I did so by myself and I put fake stage blood on him. Yes, I tore off his pyjamas and it was, "Oh, you sexy tiger." I acted out the whole scene for him, the whole works.

'Last week in court Kirk was asked where the "blood" came from on the ropes. He claimed it was my blood. Analyse it! You'll find it's Max Factor stage blood from my make-up kit.' This was the first mention of Joy's most precious resource, a magic box that rarely left her side; tools of trade that helped get her into trouble but also got her out of it; her ticket home.

By that time the magistrates had lost all thought of nudging Joy back on track. 'My little priest is quite sexually frustrated,' she told them, knowingly. 'But as soon as the ropes hit his wrists he attained sexual satisfaction.

'I just loved cooking for him, making his favourite meals, massaging his back,' she reminisced. 'I picked a romantic little honeymoon cottage because I wanted to get away from the smog of Los Angeles.

'You should have seen the place when he walked in. There were presents everywhere for him and his slippers were under the chair. I had a solid 18-carat gold ring made specially for him. It cost me over £1,000. I wanted him to have the best.

'He put his arms around my waist and kissed me on the back of the neck as I cooked. He begged me to forgive the Mormons who had done me wrong and to start afresh. Now it saddens my heart to think about the things he did at the cottage to make it look like kidnap.'

To Joy, the time together with Kirk at the cottage had been an idyll she was always ready to reminisce over. Later, when she and Keith were at liberty, they would entertain reporters who befriended them with an account of the first night at the cottage when they sat Kirk down and earnestly dissected the reasons why his sexual circuits appeared to be out of whack. They recalled the chortles with which Kirk read the scanty early reports of his disappearance. 'Hey, look, they say I was kidnapped.'

She was particularly unhappy that the police held the £1,000 ring as evidence. Dreamily, she would tell reporters, 'It was more like a bracelet or a bangle than a ring, she remembered dreamily. 'Kirk's hands were just enormous...'

Joy's story to the court was that Kirk decided to say that he had acted against his will when he realised that sleeping with Joy had once again exposed him to the retribution of the Church. When, in Devon, she had gone with him to a telephone, he asked her: 'Honey, do you mind if I tell them you forced me to come?'

Joy had been speaking for nearly an hour, passing each page as she finished reading it to Keith, beside her in the dock. The last one contained her final histrionic judgement on Kirk. 'This man has imprisoned my heart,' she said, the tears beginning to flow again, 'with false promises of love and marriage and a family life.

'He has had me cast into prison for a kidnap he knows he set things up for. I don't want anything more to do with Kirk. He does not know what eternal love is. All I ask is that you do not allow him to imprison me any longer. Let me pick up the pieces of my life.'

Then she added something that may have shown that she realised her pursuit of Kirk may not have been entirely rational. 'I ask that you let me get out of prison so I can get a counsellor to help me get over the great emotional hurt I feel inside.'

Joy was openly sobbing by this stage, gripping the dock rail. 'My father has a bad heart and this may be the last Christmas I spend with him,' she said. Then she slumped down beside Keith.

A long, wondering silence filled the court. Jackson's instinct was to bolt from the building and grab a telephone. But it was to be a while yet before the day's story could be wrapped up. The reporters could see that, magnificent as Joy's performance might have been for their purposes, it was not an entirely convincing defence against the charges she faced. Who was to say that Kirk had really been willing when he left the church with Joy and Keith? Had the guns they used – fake or not – been necessary to persuade him?

There was little chance of a firm conclusion that day. The magistrates confronted with these colourful allegations were accustomed to run-of-the-mill police cases: petty theft, minor assaults, traffic offences. Usually nothing more sexy came their way than a patient from the local mental hospital exposing himself in the street. They took rather less time than Joy had used for her speech to decide that the matter needed to be left to a full-fledged judge and jury at the Old Bailey. They committed both of the prisoners for trial.

Nevertheless, Joy's skilful and impassioned hour of pleading achieved something the defence lawyers had not been able to do during the nearly three months Joy and Keith had spent in custody. The magistrates agreed to release both of them on bail.

The reporters were still filing long after dark; long after Joy had eaten her supper of chicken and mashed potatoes – and lemonade – with Stuart Elgrod and his wife, and gone to sleep in a room without bars on the window. Jackson, pleased with his story, but parched, was headed away from the court in search of something more rewarding than lemonade when an arm snaked from a dim-lit telephone booth in the street. It was John Edwards, the passionate admirer of Joy's bosom, wrangling with a hard-pressed *Daily Mail* sub-editor who was querying something in copy he had dictated. 'What was that sentence exactly?' Edwards asked Jackson. 'You know, what she said about skiing down Mount Everest with the carnation?'

Jackson produced his shorthand note and read out Joy's imperishable words. Edwards turned back to the impatient man at the other end of the line. 'You're right,' he said. 'Make it "carnation up my nose". Take out "carnation between my nipples"…'

– 16 –

Once Joy was unconfined the Moronis of Fleet Street raised their inky trumpets and hailed her. For days the melon grin shone from millions of tabloid front pages. Proclaimed Jean Rook, super-sobsister of the *Daily Express*:

> Never had a woman laid her soul and everything else so bare, or declared her passion in such richly scented, spine-chilling language.
>
> Miss McKinney's sentence in court – 'I loved Kirk so much I would have ski-ed down Mount Everest in the nude with a carnation up my nose' – is an instant, timeless classic.
>
> It out-Juliets Juliet. Melts Women's Lib to slush. Shrivels Elizabeth Barrett-Browning's love poems to dried rose leaves. It raises Miss McKinney 29,000 ft above Emily Bronte, who was puffed by the time she reached her top with *Wuthering Heights*.
>
> In 21 poetic words, Miss McKinney snatches your icicled breath, and paints your perfumed world a passionate pink.

At the *Mirror* it could be seen from an avalanche of letters and phone calls that readers had been thrilled by Joy's star performance. Molloy kept the pot a-bubble by taking the Epsom magistrates to task in an editorial for not giving Joy bail until she had been in Holloway for nearly three months. In a page one leader the *Mirror* asked:

> What happened between her arrest on September 19 and her committal on December 11 to change their minds?
>
> If anything, Miss McKinney's situation had worsened. She now had, in their [the magistrates'] view, a case to answer.
>
> In October 1975, magistrates were advised by the Home Office to presume in favour of bail when a defendant came up on remand. The 1976 Bail Act (not yet in force) says the same...
>
> Why could the magistrates not have imposed in September the bail conditions they settled upon in December?

Never mind that without that extra time to stew in Holloway and work on her courtroom speech Joy might never have come up with the immortal carnation image.

Joy and Keith became regular visitors at newspaper offices. The saturation coverage generated by that performance in the dock made Joy and Keith, momentarily at least, the best known couple in the kingdom. They set out to make the most of their fame with the media paying the way. She coy, he sincere to the point of embarrassment, they went about insisting that what had been told in court up until then – and what was likely to emerge when they went on trial at the Old Bailey four months later – was only a fraction of the remarkable tale that they could unfold. For a price. They suggested bidding start at £50,000.

All British newspapers buy up the memoirs of celebrities. Properly promoted, a first-person story by someone in the public eye is a sure-fire circulation builder. So every editor in the Street was curious to know what Joy could possibly have left to reveal after her memorable bout of soul-baring in the dock at Epsom. But, as the literary agents with whom she flirted were also finding out, doing business with Joy was like trying to build a suspension bridge out of marshmallows. There were only two constants in her allusions to the project she had in mind. It would be packed with revelations about the Mormon Church and the Osmond Family. And: 'I'm going to be famous.'

Joy had already gone commercial, advertising in *Variety*, the Hollywood trade paper. The copy she wrote incorporated much of the self-flattery and delusion that – together with avarice – were later to be seen as her dominant characteristics.

> Attention agents and studios, Joyce McKinney, the beauty queen in the 'Mormon Kidnap Case', is writing a book and screen-play! This moving love story has taken Britain by storm, invoking front page headlines in all British newspapers. It is a tender, sensitive drama involving love, sex, religion, a beautiful intelligent girl (former 'Miss Wyoming World,' with PhD), and a handsome priest (missionary). Due to the overwhelming volume of inquiries by phone (10-20 calls per day), she is forced to look for representation. Legitimate parties please contact by letter only: Joyce McKinney, c/o Stuart Elgrod, Attorney, T V Edwards Co, Textile House, 87 High Street, Gardiner's Corner, London El 7QY, England. No more phone calls please!

Joy was a past master at Hollywood ads had anyone but known it.

This odd couple of young Americans were clearly enjoying themselves at the centre of national attention, Joy posturing like a prima donna with Keith playing the enslaved manager/companion. Everyone in the newspaper offices and television studios that they called on found them fascinating. They spoke of God more openly than most people in Britain speak of their relatives and if the talk of money became boring they were always ready to discuss sex. Even their own bewildering habits.

While Keith nodded his agreement, Joy would solemnly explain that when Kirk Anderson had taken her virginity he had thus made himself the only man in her life. Thereafter, she had saved herself for him. Keith understood this. He realised that Joy was still in love, although not with the Kirk who had accused her of a foul crime but with the Kirk who had once been her true love.

Joy needed time to make up her mind, Keith would say, tolerantly. Certainly he loved her and was devoted to her. Perhaps they would even get married one day. Meanwhile, they lived like brother and sister. Well, not exactly, they would coyly admit when teased about it. As well as reading the Bible together for an hour each day they 'did a few things'. Such as? Shyly, they admitted they did *Everything But*. At that time, only Keith knew what a wealth of possibilities Joy could bring to that situation.

The *Mirror* men and women who listened to Joy were quite candid with her. They might or might not be interested in some more of her soul-baring. They were, however, deeply interested in body-baring. In her ringing declaration from the dock Joy was actually describing what would be the Picture of the Year. What the *Mirror* – and every other tabloid in the world – wanted was a photograph of Joy. On skis. Naked. With carnation.

But it was a picture Joy insisted she would not pose for at any price. 'No *waayyy*,' she said again and again. 'No way would *Ah ever* take off *mah* clothes before a camera. *Ah* am a religious person. And it would be against *mah* Christian principles. *Mah* reputation has suffered *enough*.'

These bantering negotiations were quite tentative because, quite apart from the fact that nothing could be published until the Old Bailey trial was over, newspapers were bound by a general code of ethics that would not allow them to make payments to convicted criminals for a story – nor to people accused of crimes. Molloy and the *Mirror* lawyers felt that Joy could only be offered a contract if and when she was acquitted.

Even then there might be an obstacle. The hefty sum Joy was asking for the serialisation of the book she was supposedly writing would be negotiable. But she was also insisting on complete control of all the material, even the references to *Everything But* that she had been ready to put up as bait. The only story she was ready to see published was the version she intended to produce herself. She claimed to be deeply worried that unscrupulous 'somebodies' might fake a 'naked carnation' picture. Perhaps even the Mormons. Mormons, Joy insisted, were everywhere, keeping her under surveillance – Mormon policeman, Mormon lawyers, Mormon newsmen.

She told Joyce Hopkirk: 'Why they could put a picture of my head on another woman's naked body. Ah've heard of such things being done.' Sure enough, the *Sun*, in its extremity of desperation, would do exactly that – although a caption admitted that the picture was a composite – on the very day, weeks hence, that the *Mirror* unleashed its thunderous disclosures.

Hopkirk had been put it charge of the *Mirror*'s dealings with Joy. But she soon saw that her namesake was far more at ease with men; especially with men younger than herself. Fortunately, the first *Mirror* reporter that Joy encountered when she came out of Holloway filled the bill. Roger Beam, the one who reminded her of Kirk.

Beam, a bright, bespectacled 24-year-old, had been on the paper only a year but he had made an impressive reputation in that time, especially for tenacity. The night Joy was released from Holloway the re-united McKinney family found him planted firmly on the doorstep of their temporary home in Tufnell Park. The *Mirror* badly needed to regain the ground lost in the earliest competitive skirmishes to stake a claim of some kind on either Joy or Keith because of the editorial paralysis caused by the rift between management and journalists.

The magistrates did not sent Joy out into the world lightly. Bail was fairly low, a total of £2,500 each for her and Keith, £1,500 of it in cash. But the conditions were strict. The pair must live with Joy's parents in the boarding house where the senior McKinneys had been staying because it was convenient to Holloway. The landlady was Annette Thatcher, the 31-year-old Irishwoman who was to provide such a striking example of Joy's ruthless ability to bend people to her purpose.

Joy and Keith were forbidden to communicate with Kirk Anderson or any other prosecution witnesses; nor might they enter any premises owned by the Mormon Church. Most restrictive of all, they had to report to the local police twice daily and not leave Annette's house between nine in the evening and nine in the morning.

Although Joy's parents had been able to put up the money required to get her out of prison immediately, Keith was compelled to spend another suspenseful three days in Brixton before his parents in California came up with their contribution. He remained defiantly cheerful about the additional wait, as he had during the whole of his time in prison. He did his exercises and gave as good as he got in the heavy-handed banter that his presence attracted. 'Come on, rattle your chains for us,' the guards and other inmates would joke. They, like everyone else in Britain, were enthralled by The Case of The Manacled Mormon, as the *Mirror* had now labelled it. 'I could afford to laugh,' Keith remembered. 'I knew that I was getting out. They were staying in.'

If Keith's parents had not been able to raise the bail money the *Mirror* would probably have put it up. Reporter Barry Wigmore was sent with Beam to keep a vigil at the gates of Brixton. From then on, Wigmore's and Beam's by-lines were to be linked as closely as Joy's name was with Keith's.

Naturally enough, Beam had not been alone in waiting for Joy to return to Queen's Mansions, as Annette's establishment was known. The moment she appeared, the shabby North London street in which the house stood was dappled by the strobes of a dozen cameras. Quarrelsome reporters trying to get Joy to speak to them disturbed the peace of the neighbourhood. Not until two nights later, however, was the first blood spilled in journalistic combat – not between competing papers dedicated to each other's destruction but between the *Daily Mirror* and the *Sunday Mirror*. Stablemates.

While Keith, her comforter, confidant and quasi-lover still languished in prison, Joy had been having a wonderful time. Mr and Mrs McKinney went to Brixton to welcome Keith to freedom but Joy – Bible in hand – went out on the town with a clutch of reporters who were competing for her quotes, riding on a London bus, getting her hair done, talking about the mountain of fan mail she had received, many marriage proposals included. In the excitement of the day she fell under the sway of Peter (aka PJ) Wilson of the *Sunday Mirror*. 'I'm deeply saddened by the false image that has been presented about me,' she told him, between huge and obliging smiles. 'It's nice to be treated like the lady I am.'

Wilson, a wily operator, had made his first approaches to Joy during courtroom breaks. Now he spent the entire day flattering her into doing things his way. He treated her like the lady she said she was, even buying her some new dresses. He lured her off the bus and into in a white Mercedes hired for £40 a day. She liked that even better than her persimmon Corvette.

She arrived back at Queen's Mansions on the Friday night, firmly in the possession of PJ Wilson and his colleague Richard Moore, to find Keith awaiting, just as securely escorted by Wigmore, Beam, who had remained at the house to ingratiate himself with Annette, and photographer Harry Prosser.

The *Daily* and *Sunday Mirror* teams had an identical objective: the first picture of Joy and Keith together. Wigmore and Beam wanted it that night for Saturday morning's paper. Wilson was desperate to see that nothing appeared elsewhere before the *Sunday* could get into print a day later.

Keith, who had been made keenly aware of the *Daily*'s interest by Wigmore and Beam, was ready to repay their hospitality by co-operating. Joy listened, undecided, while the rival *Mirror* sides made their pitch.

Wilson sensed that Joy was weakening in the face of Beam's boyish blandishments. He decided on a frontal attack. If the *Sunday Mirror* was not going to get an exclusive picture, nobody would get a picture at all that night. For the Sunday, there was still tomorrow. He threw the bargaining into turmoil and his rivals into confusion by starting to shout Queen's Mansions down. 'Police!' he yelled, rampaging around the house. 'Help!'

Uproar broke out. Joy's parents fled, bewildered, to their room. Beam kept on arguing feverishly with Joy and Keith, doing his best to ignore the chaos Wilson had caused. Annette's boyfriend, a husky Greek named Mario, cleared all the reporters and photographers out of the house, still brawling and bellowing among themselves. A dispatch rider from the *Daily Mirror*, standing by to whisk film back to the office if Prosser had been able to get his shot, kept repeating to himself, 'I don't believe it. I don't believe it. They all work for the same outfit.'

Locked out of the house, Beam and Wigmore kept up the pressure on Joy with their noses pressed against her window. All right, she said eventually. 'How much?' She was learning fast. 'Will you take American Express?' Beam wisecracked back.

Joy giggled. What a dear boy!

Keith and Joy soon got into the habit of appearing at newspaper offices around meal times, ensuring that the journalists negotiating with them would fork out for costly lunches. They were touchingly unsophisticated, strangers to most of the items on the usual Londonised French or Italian menus. Neither drank alcohol. But they had an all-American fondness for good steak.

Joy had a very peculiar eating habit. She always took her own salad dressing along, a gluey concoction sticking to the sides of a screw-top bottle that she would haul from her handbag at the table. Before the startled eyes of her hosts and the waiters she would slather the stuff all over her food. Including the steak.

She did it one day to an expensive piece of meat that Alan

Shillum was about to pay for. The *Daily Mirror* news editor was not in the best of moods. He had set up a retaliatory attempt to frustrate P J Wilson's persistent efforts to get the *Sunday Mirror* its picture. Still hoping that the precious reunion shot could be preserved exclusively for the *Daily Mirror* he ordered Beam to obstruct a picture-taking session Wilson had set up in Finsbury Park on the Saturday following the shambles at Queen's Mansions,

As rival *Mirror* cars jostled for position, Beam's Mini was rammed amidships by the *Sunday*'s car, causing £200-worth of damage. The *Sunday Mirror* got its picture, though, and could afford to laugh at a sharply worded letter from the Greater London Council Parks department complaining of outrageous behaviour in a public park.

Swamping her splendid steak in gloop did much to seal Joy's fate. 'All the things that had worried me about her,' said Shillum later, 'suddenly became focused on that bit of barbarism. A woman who put that stuff on a decent steak had to have something wrong with her.'

After that fateful lunch, Joy gathered up her Bible and her salad dressing and took Keith back to Tufnell Park and the pleasures of *Everything But*. Shillum went back to the *Mirror* and told Beam and Wigmore they were to spend every minute they could spare from their routine duties delving into Joy's activities since she had first arrived in Britain.

For a couple of weeks the two reporters slipped discreetly in and out of the *Mirror* building at odd times, saying nothing to their colleagues. When Shillum heard what they finally discovered, he went to Molloy and said, 'I can't guarantee you a carnation. But it's possible that at some time McKinney posed for nude shots out in California.'

Molloy perked up. The circulation of the *Mirror* had slipped badly during the dispute and he now faced the demanding task of pushing the figures back above that of the *Mirror*'s most serious adversary, the *Sun*. A sensational development in Joy's story could go a long way towards doing it. The *Mirror* men knew that other papers would certainly be in the bidding if publication became feasible. Word had come in that Larry Lamb, the editor of the *Sun*, was ready to pay her as much as £70,000 – *if* she would also pose for the naked carnation picture.

The struggle for dominance between the *Mirror* and the *Sun*, each of which sold about four million copies a day, was the true circulation war going on in Fleet Street at the time. It was all the more bitter for being a rivalry between brothers. A lot of the men who brought out the *Sun* had learned their skills on the *Mirror*. But *Mirror* men had come to look upon their *Sun* counterparts as fallen angels, sellouts to punk journalism and circulation-at-any-cost. The *Sun* was a quintessential 'subs' paper', heavily rewritten by men who saw too little of the outside world. It had few writers or reporters of *Mirror* calibre. But the one who had been dealing with Joy from the beginning, Harry Arnold, was indisputably one of them, a dauntless and skilful antagonist whose involvement made the *Mirror* nervous. And rightly.

'California ?' said Molloy, 'Get a call in to Gavin.'

– 17 –

If everyone at the *Daily Mirror* were to be wiped out by some malignant virus planted by the *Sun*, leaving only one survivor from whom a new staff might be cloned, a single cell from Kent Gavin would do the trick. Gavin was the *Mirror* personified. Cheeky, artful, a self-made Cockney charmer. Hundreds of foreign assignments in his 15 years as a prize-winning photographer had made a cosmopolitan of him. But he would always choose the fish and chips rather than the Stroganoff. Just like the paper itself, Gavin had seen it all. But he was still readily titillated and easily shocked. Or happy to seem to be if it suited the story.

Gavin had a weakness for beauty queens. Every year when the Miss World contest rolled around and editors, numbed by the prospect of yet another cavalcade of undistinguished and indistinguishable dollops of flesh, started muttering about not covering it any more, Gavin refused to give up. Persistent as a sheepdog, he would marshal the contestants together in unexpected settings, make them dress in curious costumes. Every year he pulled off some kind of stunt that managed to lever the new batch of chicks into the paper. He was, as they say back where he comes from, a grafter.

(Anyone seeking more information on this and other aspects of Gavin's remarkable career is advised to consult his autobiography *Flash, Bang, Wallop* published in 1978 by David and Charles, Devon).

As it happened, Gavin and a reporter, Frank Palmer, were in Los Angeles at that moment, working on a more immediate *Mirror* exclusive than Joy could provide: a series about soccer stars like George Best and their high-scoring groupies. Football occupied a close second place in Gavin's heart to glamorous sex.

Naturally enough, Gavin's ever-ready eye had rested long and thoughtfully on the stories about Joy. If the picture of her that was begging so painfully to be taken could ever be arranged, he fully intended that he should be the man behind the viewfinder.

'Tell Mike I'll have a look around,' he said when he heard what Shillum had to say. 'I'll just get this Best stuff out of the way first.

Neither Beam nor Wigmore looks the way newspaper reporters are expected to look. Both wear squared-off spectacles, conventionally sharp clothes and carry briefcases. They could be accountants or bank officers. Even Mormon missionaries. But the briefcase usually contains a miniature tape recorder as well as the 'contact book' from which no reporter would be parted, any more than Joy would give up her Bible. Often as not there would be a clean shirt and a razor. No knowing where the trail might lead by midnight.

Before he came to the *Mirror* Wigmore had been chief reporter of the *Evening news*: a stand-up man. Beam had been named Young Reporter of the Year when, at the age of 19, he covered the Yom Kippur War for his provincial paper. Young though he was, Beam was to prove the most formidable reporter of all that Joy had to deal with, bringing in the famous 'getaway' pictures.

The lucky telephone call that helped Beam and Wigmore lever open their end of the story came in unsolicited. It was made by Dennis French, a North London mini-cab driver and engaging rogue who, all through the stoppage when the *Mirror*'s phones had gone unanswered, was trying to get someone to listen to the story he was busting to tell of the part he had played in Joy's escapade with Kirk.

In exasperation he had also called the *Sun*, where someone had promised to interview him but never did. He tried the *Mirror* one last time. Within minutes, Wigmore and Beam were on his doorstep, quivering like retrievers. By the time a *Sun* reporter did get around to visiting French's place he and his friend Kenny Muxlow, who had also been enlisted by Joy, had sworn allegiance to the *Mirror*. 'Sorry, chum,' Dennis told the *Sun* at his front door, as Wigmore and Beam sat nervous and silent in the living room. 'Dunno what you're talking about. I never phoned no paper. Wrong address, perhaps.'

Following up the rich bag of leads that Dennis and Kenny provided took a couple of days but soon Shillum was able to pass some leads on to Gavin and Palmer: a name and an address in Los Angeles that might or might not match; the names and descriptions of two additional American accomplices that Joy had enlisted: Jackson Shaw, a pilot, and Gil Parker, a gym instructor. Palmer settled down to the telephone in his room at their Santa Monica hotel to try to get a line on these two. Two names amid three million people. He did not even know if Gil Parker was man or woman.

Newspaper photographers are notoriously temperamental. Many would have been understandably resentful of the job Gavin had been given. Photographers like to take pictures, not search – and in this case search blindly – for pictures someone else has taken. But Gavin finished with his footballers and their nubile playmates and welcomed the chance to spend a few more days amid the temptations of Los Angeles. If there were photographs of Joy bare-assed, as he had learned to say out there, then someone must have shot them. He picked up the hefty Yellow Page section of the LA phone book and turned to Photographers. He had only Joy's real name and a single alias with which to work. A bare beginning.

By the end of the first day the *Mirror* men had each called dozens of numbers and got nowhere. They got out their rented car and drove into the city, heading for an address they had been given. They noted with some irony that the building was Holloway Manor, Holloway Drive, a large apartment block surrounded by night-blooming jasmine that as they arrived was already beginning to perfume the smoggy dusk.

The name that went with the address was Palmquist, the alias Joy had used to contact the Finlay Bureau of Investigation. Against all reasonable expectations, there it was on a nameplate by the buzzer panel. One push and they found themselves being received by the young American who – they were eventually to

113

discover – had briefly attracted attention during a break at the Epsom hearings by insulting Kirk Anderson.

It took them a little while to establish that however, since his name was not Palmquist, but Moskowitz. Steve Moskowitz. He was the caretaker of the life that Joy had left behind in the apartment where he and she had lived together, which also included Millie, the Old English Sheepdog. Joy, it transpired, had shipped Millie over to Britain, oblivious to the country's strict anti-rabies laws. The dog had been put in quarantine. Steve had paid £200 to have her flown back. In the garage beneath the building stood another relic of the happier times in Utah: the persimmon Corvette, which Steve polished and tuned regularly.

Steve, a crinkly-haired 30-year-old with a backwoods manner and a foghorn voice, was friendly. He introduced them to his new room-mate, a pretty young woman, Brigette. 'Don't get it wrong, fellers' said Steve. 'She just lives here. Helps pay the rent. We don't have a relationship. It's Joy that I'm in love with.'

Steve explained that he and Joy had met at a film club eight months earlier and become inseparable – until Keith May intruded. When Joy found herself in trouble in Britain, Steve had flown back over to be by her side – or as near to it as he could get. Then, worried that Scotland Yard might try to link him to the plot to kidnap Kirk, he had decided not to hang around.

Frank Palmer comes from the North of England and his ways are typically blunt and open. 'I don't understand that stuff between you and Joy,' he said to Steve. 'Why are you eating your heart out here if she's over in Britain with Keith? Not to mention Kirk.' Brigette offered an answer, words of wry wisdom that Joy herself might have pronounced when she was being cross-examined about Kirk. 'Baby, when you're hooked, you're hooked.'

Amiable as Steve was, he could not help with the *Mirror*'s search for pictures of Joy. Any kind of pictures. 'I'd help if I could, fellers,' he said. 'That's just what I told the other British guy.'

Other guy? 'The one from the *Sun*.' Leslie Hinton of the *Sun*'s bureau in New York, alerted by Harry Arnold, had already buzzed at the door of Holloway Manor but – apparently – not discovered anything worth reporting

Gavin and Palmer stayed with Steve for hours, pressing him gently, persuasively. They were worried about what the *Sun* might have come up with since Hinton's visit and pessimistic about their own chances of getting anywhere. They racked their brains for ways of bringing more pressure to bear on their only source. Finally, when Steve spoke longingly of wanting to be in London when Joy went on trial at the Old Bailey, Gavin offered: 'You find me the sort of picture I'm after, Steve, and I'll buy you a plane ticket.'

Jill Evans had also been fed a tip from Wigmore and Beam. Reporters don't readily part with their gleanings but the team back home could afford to be generous. They had plenty to be getting on with. What they passed to Evans put her on the road to Anaheim, south of Los Angeles, where Disneyland's make-believe Matterhorn towers over gimcrack shopping centres, one of which shelters the Christian Research Institute. Joy and Keith, it seemed, had been to the CRI several months earlier to visit the Reverend Jerry and the Reverend Marian Bodine.

This ordained couple belonged to a small task force that the CRI trained and sponsored to try to win over members of sects such as Mormons, Christian Scientists, Seventh Day Adventists and Jehovah's Witnesses to 'mainstream' Christianity. The Bodines specialised in the Mormons; their own daughter had joined the Saints and come to regret it. They believed they could show that the *Book of Mormon* was a fraud: Joseph Smith and his followers had merely plagiarised an unpublished 19th century novel and gussied it up with touches borrowed from Freemasonry.

Joy accosted the Bodines after a Sunday morning service, characteristically introducing herself by an alias – Donna – and tried to enlist their help. She poured out the story of her troubles with Kirk and how the Mormons had stepped in and sent her lover away. At that stage Joy knew only that Kirk was in Britain but not where.

'What I want,' Joy told the Bodines, 'is to find someone who really knows that Mormonism is false to go over to England with me and talk to him.' Marian recalled: 'She said we should be prepared to be away about two months. And that she would pay for the trip.'

Marian told Evans what she had thought of Joy. 'She could not be swayed from her intentions. She was not interested in any other view. I thought she was emotionally unstable. I told her that it seemed a little extreme to go to such lengths. "How do you know he will want to talk to you?" I asked. I said – and I've laughed about it since – "You can't *force* him to talk to you".'

Joy refused to give the Bodines any information about herself. 'I could understand her fear,' said Marian. 'If she knew anything about Mormon history she would know that in the early days of Utah you didn't leave the Mormon Church. You didn't tell about anything that went on in the Temple and live.'

The Bodines had even greater difficulty in understanding Keith's part in the proposed plot.

'I could appreciate Joy's attitude,' Marian went on. 'She was emotional. She was in love. She was fearful of her life because of the things she had learnt about the Mormon Church. But I couldn't see *his* connection.'

After Joy and Keith had been arrested, Keith had written to the director of the CRI, Dr Walter Martin, asking if he would testify about their intentions toward Kirk. 'We went to England and talked with him [Kirk],' Keith explained. 'And I thought that everything had been worked out. But there is one slight problem. The Mormon Church reported this as a kidnap and now we are in prison awaiting trial. We would appreciate any help or moral support you could give.'

Marian Bodine wrote the reply for Dr Martin. She and her associates were 'shocked' by what Keith and Joy had done. She remembered, too, that Joy had told her and her husband about the book she planned to write, exposing the Mormon Church and the hypocrisy of prominent Saints she had known. Especially the Osmonds.

'What are you going to say about the Osmonds?' the Bodines

had asked, intrigued. Joy pondered for a while. Then she decided that she could take these people into her confidence.

'They drink *beer*,' she said.

– 18 –

'You won't believe who's downstairs,' said Gavin, coming into Palmer's hotel room the following morning. It was only eight o'clock. Gavin had been having breakfast when the phone rang. It was Steve Moskowitz. A different Steve from the night before. No longer defensive. Out to please. 'I've got some pictures you might like', he said. 'But no one must know where they came from.'

Gavin was soon running his greedy professional eye over several sheets of black and white contact proofs. With mounting delight he realised they were illustrations of every fantasy Joy had ever laid claim to. There she was posing in an aeroplane like a 1930s film star. The plane in which she had planned to whisk Kirk away? There she was drifting in panels of white gauze. A bridal gown? A Temple robe? There she was as a cowgirl on a pony. The homemaking country girl with her lariat poised for Kirk? Finally, there was Joy as Eve the temptress. With an apple, even. Her long, long hair – a wig – romping through a forest glade, plump and a little pear-shaped. But stark naked.

Determined not to show a flicker of enthusiasm until he knew where he stood, Kent asked Steve who had taken the pictures. A photographer specialising in 'portfolios', he was told, the brochures that actresses and models assemble to show to prospective employers.

When Gavin went to the man later he said, 'I'd never been asked to do shots like those for a portfolio before. I couldn't imagine what she was going to do with them.' Nothing, as it happened. Joy never went back to pick the prints she wanted from the contacts. And she never paid the photographer his $100 fee.

Steve said, 'I don't know why everyone has had trouble finding pictures of Joy. Why don't you just follow up the advertisements?'

Advertisements? Gavin and Palmer moved in urgently on Steve. What advertisements? A few hours later the three of them were sitting, covered with dust and exhausted, in the back room of the *LA Free Press*, an underground newspaper of the kind that blossomed all over the world in the 1970s. They had found what they were looking for, buried in piles of back issues of the paper's sex services supplement, *The Freep*.

The *Mirror* had gone netting for minnows in the way of naughty-ish pin-ups of Joy but landed something of monumental fishiness. Joyce McKinney. the girl who carried a Bible wherever she went, the demure Southern Belle who shuddered at the mention of posing naked, the semi-virgin who insisted to the point of embarrassment that she had only had 'real' sex with one man, had been a call-girl. A hooker. A particularly raunchy kind of hooker at that.

Not only had Joy been Mrs Palmquist, Mrs Layton, Cathie Van Deusen and Kathy Vaughn-Bare and a few other names in which she held fake passports; not only demure Donna, when she consulted Mr and Mrs Boden. She had, Steve explained, been aka Joey – 'The Best Girl in *The Freep*'.

Little of what 'Joey' boasted being best at was left to the imagination. 'Gorgeous Former Miss USA Contestant desires work!' began the advertisement that Gavin and Palmer had unearthed from the year before. 'Beauty, Brains and Talent.' Everything Joy had ever said about herself. And more:

'PhD in Drama/Film, former model, actress, and state beauty queen, 38-24-36, a slim, sweet Southern blonde.' In Joy's unfailing way, this looked to be about half accurate in every category. The ad went on to list the delights on offer.

> How would you like HER to leisurely bathe you, lovingly blow-dry-style your hair, then give you a delicious nude massage on her fur-covered waterbed? ($100). Or try her Fantasy Room. Your fantasy is her speciality. S & M, B & D, escort service, P.R. work, acting jobs, nude wrestling-modelling, erotic phone calls, dirty panties or pictures, TV Charm School fantasies etc... *Mail* your fantasies to Joey.

An accommodation address and answering service number followed. And an afterthought: 'Upper income clientele preferred. PS. Joey says, 'Ah love shy boys, dirty old men and sugah daddies!'

The smudgy pages of *The Freep* offered a staggering insight into the sexual game parks of Southern California. Twenty-four pages of advertisements like Joy's (most of them smaller and less detailed) promised every variation on the usual themes plus a few more that the ingenuity of men and women had devised. Ludicrously, the one thing that could not be offered – because of California's anti-prostitution laws – was straightforward sexual intercourse for money. So there were offers like 'Hot and Ready. Young girls ready to come over to your place and nurse whatever needs nursing.' These were 'Outcall' services.

Under the category of 'Incall' came massage parlours galore whose ads put heavy emphasis on oral sex – giving or getting 'head', as it was described in the trade. The Suck-U-Lent Service, the Sure Thing, the Anything Goes, Charlie's Devils, the Gourmet Service. Many of the ads touted the recently fashionable sexual recreation in which American men were being encouraged to indulge. Joy emphasised these with coy capital letters: Sadism & Masochism, Bondage & Dominance. *Freep* ads even offered similar services for women, also for homosexuals. Enquirers uncertain of which category they belonged to were catered for as 'Preoperative Trans-sexuals.'

Whatever Joy could not cover on Incall – at her own apartment – as Joey, she dealt with on Outcall. As 'Misty'. Steve pointed out those ads. 'Two girls to massage, relax and pamper you,' one read. 'We are not an outcall service, just two UCLA coeds working our way through school.'

> Misty, sexy blond, 38-24-26, beauty queen, cheerleader, and Laura, foxy brunette Russian exchange student. Two girls for the price of one. Please help us pay our tuition. Call Misty...

Laura the brunette Russian exchange student? Gavin and Palmer could hardly speak for excitement. 'I'll introduce you to her,' said Steve.

The journalists never understood quite why Steve, who only a day earlier had refused to say a word to anyone about Joy's infamous past, suddenly decided to confide in them. Especially since, as they were to discover, the *Daily Mail* and the *Daily Express*, following up their own leads had also approached him before the *Sun* and the *Mirror* got around to it.

Perhaps he had suddenly realised how shabbily his devotion to Joy was being repaid. Since getting out of Holloway she had been phoning him with increasingly strident demands. It seemed to Steve that she was torn between staying in London in order to profit from her acquittal or trying to bolt in case she should be convicted. Either way, all she seemed to want from him was more and more help with no prospect, it seemed, of recognition or reward. Or perhaps it was just the companionable and reassuring confidence that emanated from this particular pair of visitors. Life had been lonely without Joy; even without Keith May.

Gavin and Palmer could feel Steve's allegiance going into reverse. Skilful as a pair of spymasters, they worked on him with sympathy and breezy cheer. Gradually they drew out the completely unsuspected spell-binding truth of how Joy had financed, equipped and planned the elaborate safari she mounted to snare the trophy of her disordered dreams.

When Steve and Joey – as he always referred to Joy when speaking of the girl in *The Freep* – had met soon after her arrival in California she was enrolled in some peripheral courses at the University of California. She had been a student for seven years by then; the identity was hard to give up. 'She told me all about the way the Mormons had treated her,' said Steve. 'And about how crazy she was about Kirk. She was ready to spend thousands of dollars finding him. And I guess I was ready to help her.'

Steve and Joy were made for each other. She wanted a slave. Partly for practical reasons, because she was going to need all the help she could get to find Kirk; partly because she enjoyed having men play the part, domination came as naturally to Joy as eating hominy grits. Steve needed a mistress. Not for sex in the customary way.

Joy's personal pleasures ran on the same lines as her business practices: *Everything But*.

'Shoot man, ' Steve assured Gavin and Palmer; 'I never screwed her. I'll bet you never find anyone who *did* screw her.'

The *Mirror* men winced and looked over their shoulders. They were sitting in a bar at the time and Steve's characteristic honk carried for yards. All through the days they spent with him he would unnerve Gavin and Palmer by unexpectedly hooting out gems of information in public places. The ears of the *Sun* might have been anywhere.

As they say in the espionage game, in which such lucky breaks are just as rare, the *Mirror* men 'turned' Steve. He became a kind of double agent, as in thrall to Gavin as he was to Joy. From that time on, everything Joy confided to Steve in her countless – reverse charge – calls, he faithfully passed on to Gavin. Long after Gavin had gone back to London these bulletins from Steve kept coming, regular as the Voice of America, 5.00 pm every Friday.

Wigmore and Beam discovered that Joy's parents had told Chief Superintendent Hucklesby about the visit to the Timpanagos Center in Provo, the psychiatric clinic that Evans had heard about but could not confirm. According to the McKinneys, she had indeed been persuaded to admit herself for treatment after the break-up with Kirk in August 1975. There was little opportunity, however, for her to receive counselling. She knew Kirk was due to begin his mission in California and the lure was too strong for her to resist. Joy had clambered out of a window of the sanatorium, loaded up the persimmon Corvette, and headed west on the trail of her Mormon priest.

This explained why Joy had disappeared from Provo so abruptly, leaving her furniture and many other things to be retrieved more than a year later. On that occasion Joy and the two men who were by then ready to do her unquestioned bidding, Steve and Keith May, were driving to Utah with her in Keith's van to retrieve the abandoned possessions when the accident occurred that left the scar on her face. She was to claim later that the mark came from an attack by a pair of Mormon thugs. But Steve's version was that he dozed off at the wheel and the van had overturned, catapulting Joy into the desert.

Joy, in fact, had given much the same story to the British investigators, adding that the insurance settlement for the injuries, $15,000, provided the money for her expedition to capture Kirk. When the *Mirror* men, who had been passed this morsel by London, mentioned it to Steve, he gave an incredulous guffaw. 'Shoot, man!' he snorted, using one of his hallmark expostulations. 'That kind of bread wouldn't have got Joey as far as the airport. She spent that much on private eyes alone, just finding out where that sucker Kirk had got to.'

At the time she met Steve, Joy had already embarked on *Freep* life, although timorously. She had done 'modelling'. Cheek by buttock with the massage parlours in Los Angeles were 'camera joints' where for $30 a time a customer got a room, a naked girl and a free film for his camera – if he had bothered to bring one. What happened behind the closed door was no concern of the management.

Joy also discovered a less demanding source of income, particularly for someone with her dramatic talents. Men were ready to pay to receive obscene phone calls. As in the *Freep* ads, she invited them to confide their sexual fantasies. She would ring them back by appointment and, in her own imaginative words, provide a replay of the visions the client had told her about while the man did whatever he wished in the privacy of his own end of the wire.

Soon Joy had half a dozen answering services picking up calls to her in as many different names. The next time Steve met the *Mirror* men he handed over a pile of telephone bills – passports to paradise in investigative terms. There, on paper, were all the calls that Joy had made for months on end and the numbers to which she made them. 'But she'd never make a call until she got the cheque in the bank,' said Steve. 'Joey wasn't in it for the fun. She wanted the money.'

The money was an additional attraction Joy held. Steve needed a room-mate to help with the rent. He was a video engineer by trade but worked as a freelance. Joy's steady income was a help. She had decided by then that her future lay in Outcall. She gave up the waterbed-equipped 'Fantasy Room' apartment she had set up to entertain her earliest clients and moved into Holloway Manor with Millie and an enormous poster of Kirk blown up from a photograph. She put the picture on the wall at the foot of her bed and, thus inspired, embarked on her personal mission.

Every week the ads – $100 a time – went off to *The Freep.* In came the calls and out went Joy, usually with Millie at her side. Her speciality had become highly sought after; she always carried her clinky little bag of chains and handcuffs.

The money rolled in, but so did the problems. Joy felt the need of more security when alone with her kinky clients than the presence of Millie, a torpid and friendly dog, could offer. Steve convulsed Gavin and Palmer by casually blurting out the solution he had contrived: 'We bugged the dog.'

Steve used his electronic skills to fit a miniature microphone-transmitter into Millie's collar. Sitting in a car outside a motel in which Joy was keeping a rendezvous, he could hear everything that went on in the room.

A second problem was that not all of Joy's clients were content with her erotic repertoire, even though it included the oral talents she was later to use with such impressive success on Kirk. For those who insisted on 'tail' as well as 'head' she decided to enlist a partner. Enter Laura the 'Russian exchange student.'

Laura, when Steve was able to persuade her to come along and talk, turned out never to have been closer to the Soviet Union than the far side of the Hollywood Hills. But she did claim to be of Russian descent – a princess by right, she insisted. She actually spoke a few words of the language. She had met Joy through her ex-husband, a Hell's Angel who had since been sent to prison for 10 years for armed robbery.

Laura, a deeply relaxed woman of about 25 with a hip style of delivery, said she always thought Joy was 'out of it... not together'.

'The girl did not even use drugs', she laughed. 'She was

naturally insane. One of the wonders of nature. Joey was on this high pedestal where she was a goddess and men have to bow and kneel to her. These customers really enjoyed a demanding female. And that is Joey. Extremely demanding lady.'

Laura rolled her eyes – one of them recently blackened in some incident of private life. 'I'm not going to lie and say I really enjoyed being around the lady because I didn't. But I really enjoyed the money. Joey took care of all the business. She checked the clients out and made sure they weren't the police. They were doctors, psychiatrists, lawyers. People with lots of time and money. Joey is an extremely good actress. One of the best.'

Laura had done her own share of acting. She had to pretend not to speak English while partnering Joy. 'Men were impressed by this. American men like foreign ladies.'

Laura had an explanation for Joy's refusal to participate fully in the sexual activities. 'She told everyone – except the clients, of course – that she was still a virgin at 26. She was saving herself for Kirk.' What would happen if a customer tried to insist on having straight sex with Joy rather than Laura? 'Joy *always* had her period. That would put them off.'

By then, though, the *Mirror* men knew that Joy was supposed to have had intercourse with Kirk. To have become pregnant by him. Or at least so she had said in court, more than once. 'Well, she told me she hadn't,' Laura insisted. She told me she had never laid him.'

Like Steve, Laura still thought of Joy by her *nom de guerre* from *The Freep.* 'In fact we worked this place,' she said, looking around.' She had met the *Mirror* men in an unexceptional hotel on Sunset Strip. 'We got $100 apiece up front to start. Joey would get the man aroused and then both of us would give him the massage. And then, you know, if the man was talking the right type of money, the man would have a little bit more. If they had enough money, the real sex would come. I was the one who got laid. Joey would, you know, orally copulate. And she was into heavy bondage. She would pull out her chains and stuff and tie the guy up.'

The additional charge was usually another $100 for Laura and $75 for Joy. Laura estimated that for more than a year they had a 'date' nearly every day – including the Sabbath – clearing $500 or $600 a week each, tax free. Joy was earning that much again from the clients to whom she tended 'solo', Steve and Laura estimated. To say nothing of the picture payments. Pictures! Gavin's stomach twitched nervously. Needfully.

Joy's discovery of Keith's invitation to fly with him in the regular advertisements of *The Freep* had turned the cosy flat-share at Holloway Manor into a *menage-a-trois*. Keith was a pushover for Joy. Just as besotted with her as Steve was, Keith decided that the way to her heart was to encourage her to play out her obsession with Kirk. He gave generous help and counsel. He also paid more than his share of the bills.

'Keith was really her duck,' said Laura, succinctly. Her duck? 'An extremely stupid, naive person that if Joey said, "Hey, look at the First National Bank. Let's go hold it up", he would hold it up. Joy was doing stuff with him but she would say it was just until she got a hold of Kirk. Their private trip was all bondage and oral sex.' The world of *Everything But*.

As Joy told her story over and over again, with only slight variations, to Steve, Keith, Laura and the other people who came to fill her new life in California, the Mormons had excommunicated her and sent Kirk into secret exile to atone for his sin. It was a harrowing, virtually operatic, human drama. The two young lovers, one a hated outsider, had become victims of their irresistible attraction to each other. The cruel Mormons had arraigned them before their congregation, publicly shaming them like medieval sinners. She had miscarried her baby, symbol of their undying love. Now the stern Saints stood like a prison wall between them, shielding the young priest from further temptation. She dared not return to Provo to look for him and any messages were bound to be intercepted. But if only Kirk knew where to find her they could fly to each other's arms on the instant.

Laura remembered Joy's grisly yarns of sexual bedevilment. A Mormon bride, said Joy, had to submit to defloration in the presence of her parents-in-law. The Saints persisted in such ancient heathen customs as the exhibiting of bridal bloodstains. This, like all the accusations Joy had heaped upon the Church, was later denied categorically by a spokesman in Salt Lake City. Jerry Cahill, the Mormon's chief public information officer, called it 'absolutely disgusting'. Nor had Joy – at that stage – been excommunicated.

At first Joy had assumed that Kirk must be in California or one of the other Western states. She had done everything she could herself to track him down, telephoning the few people in Utah she could trust. Much of the money she earned when she first began peddling her questionable pleasures in Los Angeles went on private investigators, all of whom failed to penetrate the saintly silence that had engulfed Kirk. Difficult to live with at the best of times, Joy became more and more despondent. Unbearable, even to Steve whose nature made him amenable to punishment.

Steve and Keith were easily persuaded to share Joy's indignation at the way the Mormons had treated her. Steve, the technocrat, was intrigued by her bedtime tales of ecclesiastic efficiency and greed; the genealogy bank, the huge computer that marshalled the microfilmed generations at the same time as it kept the bottomless Saintly bank-accounts balanced, tabulated the tithes and kept track of the faithful, wherever they were.

Joy and Steve hatched a superbly loony gambit. They would go to Salt Lake City and tap into the Mormon computer. Go they did, disguised, in the best tradition of Joy's operations, in wigs and spectacles. Posing as tourists they cased the Temple Square buildings and the huge LDS office block. The task was too formidable for Steve's grasp of electronics. But it put Joy on the right track. She found, or so she told a girlfriend – who later informed the FBI in revenge when Joy refused to pay up as promised for using her birth certificate for one of the fake passports – a private eye who was able to bug the Anderson home in Orem. Eavesdropping on conversations between Kirk and his mother, the investigator discovered that the young missionary was in Britain.

Joy's telephone bills took up the rest of the story. There were her calls to the Finlay Bureau of Investigation in Britain. The British gumshoes eventually found Kirk and sent back photographs of him taken surreptitiously. There were her calls to the host of heavies who had answered that final ad in *The Freep.*

When Laura and Joy teamed up, Keith took over chauffeuring Joy to and from her sessions but Millie the dog was relieved of escort duty. Once the girls had passed an hour or so with a client Keith would telephone the hotel room to announce that time was up. 'Joyce had a tendency to go over time,' said Laura. 'She would get into her bondage trip so bad. Cuffs and chains and vibrators.' When Gavin later gave Steve a guarded summary of what Laura had told him, mention of vibrators stimulated his memory. 'She was really into those things,' he said wistfully.

Laura had to shoulder more than an even partner's share of Joy's obsession. 'I got tired of Kirk and I never even met the guy. At that time Joy still had investigators looking for him. She would say, "Oh, how wonderful he was. Oh, what a wonderful body he had." I got sick of hearing his name from morning to night.

'Seemed to me that what she couldn't handle was that Kirk was the only guy who didn't *want* to make it with her. The only guy who did not want to make love with her. That was what pissed her off.'

Not the *only* guy, surely? Was this also the explanation for Joy's preoccupation with Wayne Osmond? That he had rejected her? Laura had no theories about Wayne. But memory had kicked in and there was no stopping her.

'The lady was really into sexual things, you know. She would buy the raunchiest magazines. She used to really dig watching me perform. When I would be having a client her eyes would be right down there.'

Could Laura be talking about the same girl who had begrudged the Osmond brothers a beer?

Eventually, the Finlay Bureau of Investigation came up with Kirk's whereabouts. Keith May and the other helpers Joy had chosen were briefed and she began collecting the false passports she and Keith used to enter Britain. She tried to buy the 'identity' of some other girls in the game.

After searching for more than a year she at last knew where to find Kirk and she had earned enough money – perhaps as much as $50,000 altogether – to Go Get Him.

> FREE TRIP TO EUROPE! (Big adventurous dude wanted !)
> Must be white male over 6ft 2in at least 210 lbs.
> Seeking a 'Rocky' or 'Mr Atlas' type. Prefer bodybuilder or musician.

Kirk, it seemed, was going to be either wrestled like a bull or charmed like a snake.

> All expenses paid if you help a lovely fox fulfill a unique romantic sexual fantasy-as part of her wedding party.

No one, of course, had consulted the prospective groom.

> Must be available August and September. Serious replies only! Leave message for Heidi K. at (213) 656-9353.

All aboard with Heidi aka Joy!

'I warned her that this Kirk wasn't going be glad to see her,' said Laura. 'A person that leaves you two or three years earlier, that you've only been with three weeks, is not going to say, "Oh well, glad you came to see me."'

'I used to tell her she was a fool and she would get mad. In her own mind she was convinced – once she finds him, he's going to marry her. They're going to have a little cottage with a white picket fence and children running around. You could not tell her anything different. She was so unreasonable.'

The double act was already breaking down, Laura said, because Joy had an attack of religious conscience and decided to cut down her part in the sexual antics. 'She saw God. She wouldn't even do the oral half any more. She wanted me to do *all* the work.

'I mean, the lady got so radical. The lady really needs psychiatric help. I mean, I'm not one to talk, but the lady really needs it. She's off. I said to her, "You know I love God too, but I'm not going to work my ass off every day while you take the money in".'

– 19 –

In August 1977, nearly two years after she had last seen Kirk, Joy was ready for their reunion. She bought the wedding ring for him of which she was so proud, shopped for her trousseau, paid for airline tickets for herself, the three helpers she had chosen – and Millie. Millie even had a phoney health certificate in the name of 'Billie'. There might be Mormon veterinary inspectors in Britain. Who knows?

Joy cleared out the safe-deposit box in which she kept her earnings and stuffed the money she had left into a flight bag. The bills of all denominations amounted to $12,000, give or take a couple of hundred. About £5,500.

Keith was to be one of her trio of stalwart escorts. But Steve was to stay behind at the expedition's base camp in Holloway Manor. Once Joy had matters in hand over in Britain he would, as always, do her bidding.

The other two members of the little band were Jackson Shaw and Gil Parker. Parker, an instructor at the Beverly Hills Health Club where Joy did her exercises, had pinned up the ad on the bulletin board there for her. That alone pulled in more than 70 replies and when Parker, a prime example of the kind of chap she had specified, delivered them to Joy he told her he would not mind going along himself. She ran an eye over his qualifications and said, 'Welcome aboard.'

Jackson Shaw was a horse of quite different colour. And form. He was not the catch-as-catch-can type Joy had asked for. In his early 40s, he had square-jawed good looks and man-about-California manners; something of a swinger. He was also a pilot. Joy still fancied the idea of having someone charter a plane to fly her and Kirk away from Britain to some isolated retreat. Keith had not shown a noticeable amount of good sense since falling in with Joy but he was smart enough to realise that his own flying ability was not up to the mark.

As these names were collected by the reporters, Jill Evans was pressed into service to track down these accomplices. Slogging through the distant reaches of the Los Angeles suburbs where Keith – and also Jackson Shaw – had lived she was turned away abruptly from the May door. Keith's mother made it clear she had nothing to say about her son, his companion or his present plight. Remembering that Keith had been a flier, Evans drove to the nearby airfield at Torrance, an easy going little strip of the kind that was nearly as common in California as a parking lot. Sure enough, at a flying club there, Rolling Hills Aviation Inc, owner Jan Baylor remembered Keith. While Evans watched the student Cessnas buzzing around the circuit and admired the Goodyear blimp wallowing in the smog haze over far-off downtown LA, Baylor got out the file.

Looking through it helped her remember. Keith Joseph May had flown into a little hot water at Torrance in 1975, a year or so after he became the proud possessor of pilot's licence 573983234. He took some friends for a spin and afterwards Jan had found an empty liquor bottle in the plane. She held up the chastened note he had left her after she chucked him out of the club. 'Sorry about the mishap,' Keith wrote. 'It was very bad judgment on my part.' Keith's judgment was to get worse before it got better. But he never drank while he was with Joy.

Jackson Arnold Shaw, however, was no amateur flyer; he earned his living as a pilot. Keith had only an elementary single-engine licence, but Shaw was rated for all types of aircraft, including seaplanes. He, as Evans found, was playing hard to get since his lucky escape from Joy's international flying circus. The California address he left behind in Britain had long disappeared under the concrete blanket of a freeway. His pilot's licence records carried only a post-office box number in Long Beach.

Gavin was in the grip of dismal uncertainty. What was desperately needed to clinch the *Mirror*'s revelations were pictures that proved something of Joy's raunchy past but were

131

decent enough to be published in a family newspaper. It seemed likely that there were hundreds of pictures to be harvested if he only knew where to look. There were all the shots that customers in the camera joints had taken and on call-girl jobs, clients had been allowed to snap away as they wished with Polaroids or Instamatics. At any moment some scout for an opposition paper might stumble across one of these, although by the sound of them they might be too raunchy to use. Joy had distributed glossies of herself to more or less 'straight' model agencies that had sometimes got her jobs in TV commercials or at public-relations events. Steve had described piles of those portfolio pictures littering in the Holloway Manor apartment but in one of her regular phone calls from London – for which Steve always paid – Joy had ordered them destroyed. The thought hurt Gavin's stomach.

But Steve had also told him that Joy modelled for titles whose standards were less lofty than those of *Playboy* or *Penthouse.* She had been particularly insistent that he get rid of all the copies of these from the apartment. And did you? Gavin asked, his innards churning with anxiety. Not all of them, Steve admitted. After sifting through the little cache of magazines hidden away in the garage, Gavin knew where to go looking.

Just where Joy had often swung the Corvette out of Holloway Manor to drive east along Santa Monica Boulevard, a huge sign proclaims that *Hustler* magazine was 'For Those Who Think Pink'. 'Going pink' was the technical term that the flesh magazines, of which *Hustler* was king, used for the only frontier that remained, once they had made the big break through the pubic hair barrier.

The beginning of that stretch of Santa Monica was medium elegant. Rolls Royce servicing. Poodle grooming. The Beverly Hills Health Club (where, alas, no one had any idea what had become of Gil Parker after he signed on with Joy). The elegance soon petered out, giving way to the gaudy facades of establishments like the Pussycat Theatre and the World Famous Paris House Nude, the 'modelling' centre where Joy had once been a *specialité de la maison.*

132

Inside one of the converted shopfronts across from the Paris House, Gavin found Al Guthu, a man who looked as though he was waiting for someone to shoot a television series around him. The lights were low. One corner of the office was given over to a large cockatoo in a cage.

A telephone rarely left Guthu's hand. He was an agent. The girls whose pictures studded the wall were models and actresses whose careers were just beginning in the pages of *Hustler* and its lesser imitators. Or just ending. Most of their portfolios looked like gynaecology manuals.

Sure, said Al Guthu, he knew Joy, Heidi. Misty. Whatever. Most of his clients had their akas. In this business... you know? Gavin was learning. He already knew how to be persuasive. And business-like. Guthu produced his record books with the names of the photographers to whom he had sent Joy.

Gavin was not quite sure what to expect from a magazine called *Chopper*. But it turned out to be about motor-bikes. The girls on or beside the machines in its pictures were only incidental. Editor Chuck Dagion had personally shot the pictures of Joy that they used. 'I remember,' he said 'she brought her dog with her. She kept on about being on the run from Utah and about the Osmond family. I thought she was a kook. I gave her around $80 for that day's work.'

Dagion took to Gavin just as Steve had done. They made a deal. The *Mirror* would give *Chopper* whatever pictures it wanted of Joy's activities in London in exchange for the entire set of colour transparencies that Dagion had shot during his session with her.

The pictures that had been published were unexceptional. Joy was not entirely naked, although the celebrated, guaranteed authentic, bosom was fully on view. The shoot had been back in 1976, Bicentenary Year, and she had been dressed up in costume to commemorate the Boston Tea Party.

Gavin was more interested in the frames that had not been published. Joy had been Thinking Pink all right. The melon grin beamed saucily out over her splayed, naked thighs. What *was* she doing with that teabag?

Gavin was quite shocked. But happy. The *Chopper* pictures left no doubt about one thing: Joy was a natural blonde.

Barbara Dragin also took her own pictures. She ran not one magazine but eleven; all devoted to one of Joy's specialties, the newly fashionable sexual sport of bondage. They had titles like *Knotty* and *Hogtie*. She too remembered Joy well. Obligingly, she gave Gavin the model release form Joy had signed for a layout in one of the magazines, *Bound to Please*. Lexi Martin – yet another aka.

Sure, Dragin would sell Gavin the pictures. And what a mind-boggling set they were. There was Joy, unmistakable, even in dark wig, miniskirt and boots, acting her heart out in a sequence in which another girl was energetically maltreating her. For nine pages of 'crotch shots' and simulated anguish, Joy lay sprawled on a make-believe hospital bed, gagged and writhing, pulled this way and that by bonds and 'restraints'. Those years of drama lessons had been put to profitable use.

The caption read: 'No! the bound girl protested, when her leather blouse was opened, revealing her full upstanding breasts.' Upstanding Joy's certainly were through the gaping bodice, even while she was lying on her back. Too upstanding, to Gavin's cultivated gaze. The camera's cruel eye picked out the unmistakable tell-tale scar on the underside of each splendid globe where the plastic surgeon's scalpel had opened an incision and slipped in the little sacs of silicone. The legendary bosom Joy had so insistently declared to be all her own was not authentic after all.

Yet another photographer who produced some nudes of Joy, Al Gaulgan, told Gavin, 'She used to come here with her dog. She worked two months for me and did about 12 assignments – two of them for bondage magazines. About April '76 she suddenly decided she wanted her fee doubled.

'I couldn't pay her. She quit and placed her own adverts. When I tried her later with more work she was too busy with jobs she had found herself. She always said that one day she would be rich and famous.'

Gavin did not know about rich. But he could promise Joy fame of a kind. The pictures and the story that Palmer was writing were dynamite. If the *Sun* or some other paper were to swallow the tale of innocence and victimisation that Joy was hawking around Fleet Street, the *Mirror* would blow it out of the water with the explosive truth. Whether Joy was acquitted or convicted of kidnapping she would be exposed as a pious and preposterous fraud.

With a combination of guile, generous fees and exclusive contracts, Gavin spent three days gathering up all the pictures he could find, carefully closing every door against other seekers of truth – like the *Sun*. He spent an entire afternoon negotiating for a splendid set of Joy in black suspender belt and undies wrestling with an Oriental girl. But he was haunted by the knowledge that there must be hundreds more pictures in existence of Joy doing all kinds of things and that he would never be able to collect them all. If he had not had to get back to London he might easily have become as obsessed by his quest as Joy with hers for Kirk.

Despite all the effort he had put in, Gavin's most pressing obligation at that time was delivering the pictures for his sexy soccer series. Neither he nor Palmer had said a word to the office about the pictures they had collected. The fewer people who knew the better, even close colleagues. They assumed from what they had been told that there was plenty of time in hand before it might be possible to publish anything about Joy. They had the goods on her though, for when that moment came. Later that night while the *Mirror* men were drinking to celebrate their triumph, they showed the bondage pictures to Steve. Tipsy tears began to flow. 'Oh, my little Joey,' he crooned over the shocking images. 'Why did you do it?'

Never a one to miss taking advantage of someone's weak moment, Gavin asked him, 'What about that baby, Steve? The baby Joy said she was going to have with that Mormon bloke. Was she really pregnant?'

'Shoot man,' said Steve, 'She used to miss periods even though she never had sex. I think she made it all up.'

– 20 –

Back in London it was taking Wigmore and Beam a little time to gain the complete confidence of the informants who had so fortuitously fallen into their hands, Dennis French and Kenny Muxlow. Eventually, after a series of delicate meetings with the pair, the reporter got a call from a third Englishman named Alan Austin, who had recruited them for Joy.

To get Austin to cooperate Wigmore and Beam needed to be as persuasive as Gavin at his best. They were afraid of losing their exclusive grip on the London end of the story. They knew that the *Sun* was keeping an eye on their moves. These three crucial contacts could all too easily be tempted out of the *Mirror*'s grasp. For the moment, though, at a series of meetings in a colourful East End pub, The Charleston, in Stratford East, Austin and the other two gradually unfolded their uproarious tale. It could well have been entitled *Joy and Keith Meet the Lavender Hill Mob*.

When Joy and her Californian entourage flew into Heathrow on 5 August 1977 only Keith and herself had an inkling of the lengths she was ready to go to in landing Kirk. In one of her eight suitcases was a pair of handcuffs given to her by an LA detective who had been accepted as an *Everything But* client.

The party ran into difficulties even before they entered Britain officially. While Joy was sailing through one line of immigration inspectors using the passport proclaiming her to be Mrs Layton, Gil Parker, the muscleman, was running into difficulties in another channel. Joy, who had warned all the men not to seem as though they were with her, had the shoulder bag of cash. Parker had only a few dollars on him. The immigration man's questions, particularly about how he proposed to support himself in Britain, made him nervous. He got cold feet. 'Forget it,'

Parker told the others when they reassembled. 'I'm going home.' He booked a plane back to LA for the next day.

Britain seemed a long way from California and the local habits were strange. Joy soon realised that she was going to need some expert local advice. Jackson Shaw, the pilot, had a flying friend in London who might be able to help – Alan Austin.

So far as Austin could make out Joy was just a wacky American planning herself a somewhat far-out wedding, cost no object. After she had gone to the bank to change her dollars for pounds she mentioned that she was going to need a couple of cars. Austin put them in touch with his pals. 'What do you do in a situation like that?' Austin asked the enthralled *Mirror* men. 'I thought the first time I met these two – blimey, I've got a right couple of nutcases here. I mean they don't even drink!'

Joy could not have chanced upon a more willing pair of helpers than Dennis and Kenny. Dennis, a hulking 24-year-old with a streetwise chirpiness and a colourful past, chortled, 'Joy had thousands of pounds to spend – so we thought we'd help her.

'There was this crazy bird wandering around with a sackful of money. It was all new £20 and £10 notes, still in their bank wrappers. They were throwing it about left, right and centre. They were a real easy touch. We conned them rotten.

'She wanted a car. It had to have automatic drive. She couldn't work gears.' Dennis and Kenny went to a backstreet car dealer and bought an old Austin Westminster limousine for £75. 'I thought I'd sell it to her for £160,' said Dennis. 'But when she saw it she flipped. I did a heavy selling job, showed her the pull-down picnic tables in the back. Told her what a smooth car it was. 'I said I'd let it go for £275. She said "Sold" and paid for it there and then in cash, all tens and twenties. She was like a kid with a new toy, stroking it and saying how beautiful it was.'

Kenny, who had spent a goodly part of his 25 years collecting tattoos as well as a variety of mischievous ways, was fascinated by Joy's sharply focussed preparations for her honeymoon. He drove her to buy the tape player for the music that was meant to remind Kirk of their First Time, back in Provo. She insisted that they pop into a sex boutique where she bought some creams and a spray called 'Stud' that was supposed to help sustain erections. 'Amazing stuff,' said Kenny, who had not been able to resist trying it out. 'I lasted for three hours.'

Away from Dennis and Kenny, who were the mere foot soldiers of the expedition, Joy and Keith went on the town with their senior advisors, Austin and Shaw. Joy always paid, plucking notes from her bottomless bag.

One night in a boisterous West End restaurant Joy, feeling overheated, hauled off her sweater. The twin treasures that swelled beneath her see-through blouse caused a sensation for several tables around. Austin, who had introduced the others to the place, became nervous 'If anyone gets fresh,' he said, 'throw a coat over her. We don't want a fight.'

Austin had been mightily impressed by Joy's assets. 'She was all woman,' he said. 'That bust is all hers. She never wears a bra and she swears that nothing is artificial. She told me she does exercises every day to keep them firm.' Gavin would have enjoyed his simple faith.

Austin was also impressed by Joy's other outstanding abilities. 'She was no dummy,' he said. 'She was a master of disguise. With those wigs, make-up and glasses she used to use her own mother wouldn't recognise her.'

Shaw was the first to suspect that Joy and Keith might be headed for real trouble when he saw a side of Joy he had not been aware of. Soon after their arrived in London, she heard somehow that the Mormon church in Orem had, in fact, announced her excommunication. The news triggered a full-blown tantrum, a blast of threats against the Saints. Shaw didn't like the sound of that. He had come along strictly for the ride. He told Joy and Keith he was going on a little trip to visit some friends and never came back.

Shaw's defection put an end to Joy's prospects of whisking Kirk away by air to a secluded love-nest in Ireland or on the Continent. But it would have needed more than that to daunt her ambitions, now that she was so close to assuaging the thirst that had drawn her half-way around the world.

Dennis, too, began to wonder if Joy was really playing with a full deck. 'She suddenly whipped out this photograph of Kirk Anderson,' he said. 'She says: "This is my lover. I'm going to carry him off." I was dumbstruck. I didn't know what to say, it was so crazy. If you'd met those two at that time you'd never think they were capable of anything like that. They were such a pair of dummies. Anyway, she goes on to tell me that even if she can't marry this bloke she wants a baby from him.'

Dennis had loved that. 'I says: "Why go to all this bother? I know dozens of blokes who'll give you a kid for nothing. If you can have kids, they'll guarantee it in one night."

'Then Joy tells me this story about how she had Kirk in bed one day. They'd been fooling around and got each other excited. She was all ready to make love when all of a sudden Kirk jumps out of bed, pulls on his trousers and kneels down and starts to pray.

'Joy told me: "He asked God to forgive him for what he'd done." I was laughing all the time – I couldn't believe my ears.' Interestingly, Joy did not tell Dennis that she and Kirk had actually made love or that she had become pregnant.

Joy and Keith set out house hunting. Dennis and Kenny drove them further and further afield. At first they were looking for somewhere with barred windows. Joy explained to Keith that there was always the danger that Kirk would get it into his head that she had been sent by the devil and take off. When they settled on the Oakhampton cottage she decided to reinforce the windows with bullet-proof Plexiglas. A St Albans glazier quoted £70. Joy dug in her bag.

The plan moved into top gear. There was more driving around London in search of a waterbed. Joy wanted to reproduce the scene from Provo that she remembered with such vividness exactly. The fur rug, another vital prop, she had brought from California in her luggage.

London waterbeds were too expensive. Joy bought the biggest double bed she could find and had it sent down to Devon together with a new refrigerator. If Kirk was going to sin he was going to go the whole hog, drinking Cokes as well as having sex.

She bought sheets in Kirk's favourite blue and had them

monogrammed. She bought him a silk dressing gown and the pyjamas that were later produced in court, shredded. Only when Keith asked to be driven to a hardware shop in Archway, where he picked out the chains with which Kirk was to be restrained, did it dawn on Dennis and Kenny that they were dealing with something more than mild transatlantic eccentricity.

Dennis's misgivings deepened when he took Keith to a locksmith and watched him buy one of every size of padlock the shop had in stock. He added in a four-foot length of chain and another of six feet, with links as thick as a man's thumb, that was later used to chain Kirk to the bed. The shop assistant asked: 'What are you locking up tonight – the Crown Jewels?'

Unknown to these local accomplices, the day set to swoop on Kirk came closer. Joy found the tension harder to bear. Meeting her and Keith one day Austin opened the back door of the car in which she was sitting and, to his embarrassment, found her with a coat across her knees and her jeans around her ankles. He had interrupted something. 'She just said, "Come in",' he recalled. 'Keith got really mad with her. He was jealous that she would flaunt herself that way.'

Finally Dennis and Kenny became spooked by their clients' erratic ways. They took Joy and Keith for a last ride and while they were out of the car just drove away. Austin, too, fell out with the Americans shortly before they launched their big operation because Joy finally woke up to the financial liberties his two friends had taken with them. Despite what they themselves were plotting to do, Joy and Keith went to the police to complain. Austin's version was: 'After an argument over money that Joy thought had been stolen, I decided I wanted nothing to do with them. They reported me to the police, so I told detectives about their forged passports.'

That was just *after* the news had broken of Kirk's disappearance. Why had he not reported them before that? 'How could I tell the police that two young Californian tourists were planning to shanghai a Mormon missionary for love? They'd have laughed in my face.'

Later, when news reports of the alleged kidnap mentioned a

'Bob Bosler', Austin recognised it as one of the names Keith had been using. He rang Mill Hill police station and told them: 'Remember those forged passports? Well those two who had them got the Mormon.'

Alan went on: 'For my troubles the law hauled me out of bed at 6.30am the following Saturday and arrested me as a suspect. Eventually the police apologised about the passports. They said: 'You were right. We've checked with America and they're definitely dodgy.'

As Keith May had been subverted, so Beam and Wigmore 'turned' Austin. Jackson Shaw had gone to ground in California from where he would frequently call his old friend to see if he was in danger of being linked to Joy and Keith. Whatever Shaw told Austin went straight to the *Mirror* reporters. Occasionally Beam and Wigmore would test these circuits they and Gavin had set up by feeding a scrap of information in one end and waiting for it to come out the other. Wigmore to Austin, Austin to Shaw, Shaw to Steve, Steve to Joy, Joy to Beam. Or Beam to Joy, Joy to Steve, Steve to Gavin. The *Mirror* missed nothing – until Joy's final, shattering, leap to freedom.

Out on bail, her operating fund depleted by her experience with British helpers, money became a priority for Joy. She knew her story – even Keith's – was worth a lot if they were acquitted. They had become household names. A pop group in the Midlands called itself The Joyce McKinney Experience, its girl lead singer belting out *Love Songs For Kirk*. The Church of Latter Day Saints found that far from its name being besmirched by Joy's assertions about it, the number of people interested in becoming Mormons increased. Richard Eyre, who turned out to be, in real life, a marketing consultant, produced a 19-year-old missionary working in Oxford to testify. 'People who wouldn't normally talk to us,' said Bruce Derrick, 'now seriously want to discuss doctrines they first heard about from the court case.'

Joy and Keith were constantly assured by representatives of every great national title that the odds were heavily against any jury agreeing that the police were right to charge them with such serious offences. Once she had been found not guilty Joy could, within reason, name her own price. Sometimes the papers went to her; just as often, Joy and Keith called on them. On one of her flirtatious negotiating visits she was actually being entertained in Mike Molloy's office at the *Mirror* when Kent Gavin arrived from Heathrow Airport and strolled in.

Joy's presence in the building was a measure of the fascination this weird and wondrous creature had come to hold for Britons. People from other offices drifted in and out, on some pretext, to get a good look at her as she sat demurely, drinking her Coke.

She had been telling everyone how the Mormons were out to blacken her reputation, the melon grin flashing its appeal, the blonde lock constantly patted against the scar on her jaw. She had just posted off the letter to the *Avery Journal* that told of the harsh treatment she had received in Holloway and continued:

> Now after only a preliminary hearing, British sentiment is on my side! All the television shows are wanting to interview me, and three publishing companies want to buy my life story. On Monday a film director is flying out from LA to talk to my lawyer...
>
> No doubt reporters and other strangers will continue coming to Avery County, questioning you people about me, trying desperately to dig up any scrap of dirt they can.
>
> Beware my friends, for they are wolves in sheep's clothing! They will take your words and twist and distort them and change them in print. I urge you strongly to PLEASE say ONLY good things about me for my whole reputation and future are at stake. Anything you say will be printed. My former fiancé was quite perverted in his hangups, but he tried to put the blame for his perversions off on me – so the reporters may question you carefully as to my morals, and they will try to get you to degrade me. I urge you to tell them the truth: that my nickname in high school was 'Iceberg', that I was boy-shy, and seldom dated (I was more the studious type) and didn't even play kissing games at parties. Also that I was never known to smoke, drink or use any type of drugs or profanity and that I come from a good family. Also that I represented Avery County in the 'Miss North Carolina High School Contest' as 'North Carolina's ideal high school girl', as well as being a North Carolina 'Junior Miss' and later 'Miss Wyoming' in the 'Miss USA' pageant. An important point to tell them is that I was (and still am) a Christian girl – very active in church (singing, giving inspirational readings, teaching Sunday School classes when needed, and attending Christian service camp).

All through high school and college I had top grades. These things won't be bragging about me – they will just be emphasizing the positive aspects of my personality rather than the negative things said by the press in the past.

It was the first time Gavin had seen Joy in the flesh, although by now he was familiar with every blossom and blemish on her body. He joined in the general chat about what Joy might eventually include in the story she was promising and how it might be projected. Inevitably, he asked her about the carnation on skis picture of which he and every other photographer in Fleet Street still dreamed. Joy responded haughtily '*Ah* simply will not pose nude,' she said, with an imperious wriggle of her bosom. 'Ah never have. And ah *never* will.'

'Pity,' said Gavin, drumming his fingers on the heavy manila envelope he had nursed all the way from Los Angeles.

Joy was even available for stunts. Peter McKay, the impish spirit behind the *Daily Express* celebrated William Hickey column (named for a notorious 18th century diarist), looked over an invitation to the premiere of a Joan Collins film, *The Stud,* and guessed that if Joyce McKinney could be persuaded to go along and share the spotlight with London's glitterati, not only would the occasion be considerably enlivened but he would have a fine lead for the column. Joy found the prospect irresistible, especially once she saw who was to be her escort for the evening, McKay's colleague, Peter Tory.

In some ways Tory exemplified a certain kind of young man who drifted in and out of the fanciful world of gossip-writing: presentable, able to turn a neat phrase, well-connected – his father was a distinguished diplomat – but unfettered by scruples about undermining the establishment or exploiting a friendship. However, there was more to Tory. He had been an actor for some years, a member of the Royal Shakespeare Company. He was a flier; owned his own vintage aircraft. When that came up in conversation, Joyce seemed *very* interested.

'Hire a Rolls-Royce,' McKay told Tory. 'Give her the full treatment. They'll love it out there.' He was right. Tory picked Joy up at the north London house, the Rolls blocking the grim narrow street, half the neighbourhood turning out to gasp. They arrived at the floodlit Leicester Square cinema early, the driver sliding into the line of limos pulling up at the top of the red carpet. Tory, suave and slender in a dinner jacket, helped Joy out of the car, making sure to swing her spectacular full frontal exposure towards the fans behind the barricades.

So celebrated had Joy become that London's nightlifers were more enthralled by her than by the stars tripping by ignored.

Even the real celebrities were keen to be introduced. She signed autographs right and left, flashed her blinding smile. The photographers swooped; the *Express* got its pictures of Joy among the stars. The strobes faded swiftly as soon as rival cameramen realised what was going on but that didn't matter to Joy. She was where she always dreamed of being; at the centre of a glamorous throng at a great media occasion.

When the film was over, she and Tory effortlessly gatecrashed the reception. Barrister Ami Feder, briefed by Stuart Elrod, had persuaded a sympathetic judge to ease the bail conditions and she was now allowed to stay out late. There was no reason to doubt that Joy and Keith would appear for their trial, Mr Feder said. 'She wants to remain in this country to clear her name.' The application went unopposed and the pair were told they need only report to a police station once a day rather than twice.

At the party Joy pouted and fluttered, danced, drank her Coke, flirted with actors – even with a waiter she mistook for one. Going home in the Rolls, Joy peppered Tory with questions about the people she had met, thanked him with a kiss on the cheek. There was not the slightest sign that this was her farewell appearance. Poor old Keith, Tory realised afterwards, must have spent the evening packing the getaway bags.

When Joy was seen to have jumped her bail, Jean Rook wrote in the *Daily Express*:

> Not-so-dumb blonde, Joyce McKinney, flees the country in purple sunspecs, a red wig and a pom-pom hat. It's a tragedy we let her slip and in National Smile Week, too. Flawed or not, that girl is a priceless gem and an incalculable loss to anybody.

At first it seemed that the greatest loss would be suffered by national editors and circulation directors. At the *Mirror* though, Molloy had watched the *Express*'s premiere stunt with quiet pleasure. He assumed it was the opening stage of a courtship that would eventually result in Joy being offered an irresistible proposal. The *Express* had a new editor, Derek Jameson, who until recently had been managing editor of the *Mirror*, effectively Molloy's deputy. He was out to make his mark at the helm of a rival title and the McKinney story, if a way could be found to tell it, might easily do it for him. The *Mirror* had always hoped it would be the *Sun* that walked into the trap that the offer of Joy's story represented. But the *Express* would do almost as well.

When Molloy ushered Joy out of his office after introducing her to Gavin he had little idea of what Gavin had unearthed in Los Angeles. Fearful of leaks, and under no immediate deadline pressure, all the *Mirror* men and women working on the story had been excruciatingly cautious: never a word in phone calls or messages to the office about developments or contacts. Home phones, however, rang late into the night; Beam and Wigmore had furtive encounters with Shillum in pubs far away from the *Mirror* building. Joy and Keith were still on their way down in the lift when Gavin opened his envelope and spread the sensational finds all across the floor of Molloy's office. More than 300 images of Joy in all her undeniable glory.

'It was like opening a chest of pirate treasure,' Molloy remembered. 'In circulation terms, we were looking at pure gold.'

The strategy the *Mirror* devised was based on the assumption that Joy would stand trial on the appointed date, 2 May 1978, and once there had been a verdict it would be able to publish a week-long series, unfolding day by circulation-building day. Even if either of the Americans was found guilty the *Mirror* would not have paid a cent and would not, therefore, be rewarding criminal activity. All it had to do was to keep the priceless asset represented by the pictures and the reporters' stories under wraps until the moment came.

If some rival paper were to hand over a large sum for the sanitised account that would be all Joy was likely to agree to – something like *The Greatest Love Story Ever Told* – then all the better. The *Mirror*'s authentic version would not only sell far more papers it would cost the duped rival dearly in money as well as prestige. Under the guise of preparing a huge promotion drive for the soccer star series, the *Mirror* organised a budget for television advertising, and briefed its circulation and production departments.

146

With Joy's disappearance three weeks before the trial date the bottom dropped out of the *Mirror*'s plan. The most that could be done immediately was to break the story of the getaway and illustrate it with pictures that, Molloy decided to say, had arrived in the post, together with a small collection of the death and birth certificates Joy had used to get fresh passports. The evidence had actually been produced by Roger Beam, who politely declined to say where he had got it. Shillum and Molloy refrained from pressing him for an explanation but the stuff could only have come from Annette Thatcher. Two polaroids of the absconders in overblown disguises – dark wigs, huge spectacles, Keith with a false moustache – made a fine front page but it did not dispel the chill of disquiet running down the spines of the *Mirror* team in the know. A Fleet Street pack would soon be on the fugitives' trail and who knew what might be uncovered that would render the *Mirror*'s precious scoop worthless?

There was danger also from within. The head of the *Mirror* legal department told Molloy: 'If you publish a word of the material you have prepared, and above all those scandalous pictures, the paper will receive a heavy fine and *you* will almost certainly go to prison.' There was every likelihood, Powell emphasised, that the absconders would be extradited from the United States, or wherever they were found, eventually to stand trial. In the meantime, nothing could be published that might influence future jurors.

That did not mean, however, that the hilarious story of the couple's escape could not be pieced together and told. It was clear that Joy had been planning for quite a while to jump her bail. Steve assured Gavin in his regular bulletins from Los Angeles that he had heard nothing from Joy since a few days before she bolted. But the *Mirror* began to suspect she may have picked up some miniscule vibration that made her fear Steve's loyalty was on the wane. It seemed that at the last she had come to trust only Keith and her new recruit, the former landlady, Annette.

Familiarity with Mormon ways meant Joy had known just where to look for a name and a set of vital statistics to apply for the new passports. Accompanied by Annette, she put on a wig – old stuff for her – and headed for the building in Exhibition Road where the Mormons had established a genealogical 'bank' to help British converts track down ancestors who would benefit from post-mortem conversion to the faith. Annette, claiming to be a devout seeker, and Joy, posing as a Swede to disguise her accent, soon had what they needed. Joy insisted the birthdates for the long-departed whose identities were to be adopted must be exactly the same as hers and Keith's.

The morning after Joy's evening on the town with Peter Tory she and Keith had gone to West Hendon police station for the daily check-in that was a condition of their bail. Then, out came the make-up case and the wigs. Spectacles too.

Hardly inconspicuous, since they had seven trunks and suitcases with them, the absconding pair took a taxi to Paddington station then, to confuse the scent, another cab to Heathrow Airport, where they were booked on a British Airways flight to Shannon, in Ireland. At 2.30pm they flew out of Shannon to Toronto on Air Canada. They used British passports in the names of Joan Anne O'Connor and Anthony Peter McGowan, obtained by using the certificates based on data from the Mormon archives that eventually found their way into Beam's hands.

At Shannon, Joy spotted an opportunity to deepen the deception. A deaf-and-dumb mime troupe was checking in at the same time. She and Keith switched to silent mode, scribbling notes to make check-in staff think that they, too, were unable to hear or speak. It worked so well that Air Canada decided not to make them pay excess for their pile of luggage. They were assumed to have slipped into the United States at nearby Buffalo.

With the elaborate plans that had been shaped around the assumption that Joy would be acquitted thrown into disarray, Molloy needed advice. In the view of journalists, newspaper lawyers are divided into two groups. One follows the natural inclination of the calling and looks for reasons that a story should not be published. The other group, a cherished minority, strives to find ways in which a risky story can be made safe for publication. Hiram Powell, the *Mirror* legal manager, belonged firmly in the first group.

Powell offered much the same opinion that had been brought back by the *Mirror* men who had gone down to the Old Bailey in the remote hope that Joy might show up. The prosecution and defence lawyers shuffling off to disrobe had been unanimous that until Scotland Yard discovered the whereabouts of Joy or Keith and the Director of Public Prosecutions decided whether or not to extradite them, any publication that could influence the jury in a re-scheduled trial must be withheld. It was Powell's uncompromising view that the disclosures the *Mirror* was poised to make fell into that category. Not a word from the thick dossier the reporters had so painstakingly compiled, and certainly not a single one of the devastating pictures Gavin had collected, could be published.

Molloy's relationship with Powell and his colleagues, two more barristers in the *Mirror*'s employ, was delicate. The principle governing it was: lawyers advise, editors decide. Legally speaking, an editor was responsible for everything his paper printed; legally, Molloy was the personification of the *Mirror*. The lawyers' view – Powell's colleagues agreed with him – was not binding, but it could not lightly be ignored. An expensive lawsuit would not endear an editor to the board of directors that in Molloy's case included his predecessor Tony Miles, who was now the group's editorial director, effectively editor-in-chief of all the *Mirror* titles.

Paying out legal damages or fines, to say nothing of hefty costs, would be a grave enough consequence if a judge or the DPP decided there had been contempt of court. Being locked up would obviously be a good deal worse. It was a sensitive issue at the *Mirror* because some thirty years earlier one of Molloy's predecessors, Silvester Bolam, had achieved the distinction of being the only national editor in living memory to be given a prison sentence for contempt.

The *Mirror* did have a couple of valuable advantages: the pictures of Joy and Keith in their ludicrous escape outfits and the documents from the Mormon archives. They made a splendid page one splash but the huge circulation lift that the real Joy story would guarantee needed the day-after-day impact of a revealing series.

Abrasive arguments raged around the *Mirror*. Everyone involved in getting the story begged Shillum to prevent their efforts going to waste. The public were entitled to know the truth, the journalists insisted. The alleged kidnapping itself was not at issue so why were the lawyers being obstructive? Shillum beseeched Molloy. Gavin, too. Molloy shut them all out of his office.

Gavin was still hearing from Steve. There had still been no word from Joy but opposition reporters had tracked down his phone number and were calling. Gavin coached him in how to mislead them – especially the *Sun*'s Harry Arnold.

What Molloy desperately wanted was some signal that Joy would not be coming back to Britain and that, therefore, there would be no trial. Or – perhaps even better – that a rival paper would find her and be ready to take the risk of publishing whatever she might tell them. If other newspaper lawyers would be bolder than those at the *Mirror* he could justify the risk of opening the floodgates. Every day that passed lessened the chances of keeping his great scoop watertight. Even if there were no leaks from inside the *Mirror*, the teams that every other paper had scouring likely parts of the United States were bound to make their own discoveries. Molloy did not really care who found the absconders, just so long as someone did.

Even though no one in authority would say so, Fleet Street soon began to suspect that there was little likelihood of Joy ever coming to trial. Discreet but persistent enquiries by reporters produced the impression that the judicial authorities and – especially – the police would be happy never to hear of Joyce McKinney again. Still, judges and judicial bureaucrats were notoriously unsympathetic to the popular press and editors could easily imagine a swipe from the sword of justice coming their way.

At the *Express* Peter Tory was taking Joy's disappearance personally. He was annoyed, not just because Joy had used him to flaunt herself so deceptively at the premiere he had taken her to but because he thought his professional instincts might have been clouded by the euphoria of the event. Should he have given Joy a heftier grilling about her plans? Did he fail to pick up on some hint that she was planning a flit? When the switchboard asked if he would accept a reverse charge call from Miss Stud, and he heard the familiar breathless voice at the other end, he mustered all his actor's charm and wiles.

Joy and Keith were indeed back in the United States. They had reverted to their own American passports and gone across the Canadian border without any problem. Since then they had kept on the move. They seemed genuinely afraid that they would be tracked down by the FBI. Joy was also puzzled, even a little disappointed, that the American media had not been more impressed by their flight from British justice. She was feeling neglected.

Tory was not to know that Joy had also been phoning the *Mirror* – collect, of course. She wanted to talk to her erstwhile favourite, Roger Beam. He tried to string her along, assuring her that the paper was still interested in making a deal with her when it was possible to do so. But she was impatient with him; petulant. The romance was over.

More calls came in *to the Express* from Joy as she and Keith meandered from state to state, and eventually Tory was confident enough to stride into Derek Jameson's office and say that Joy was ready to do business.

Even more than Tory, Jameson felt that the fates were with him at that moment. He had barely been in the editor's chair long enough to warm the seat and he needed something to help him make a spectacular debut. After a season of discontent in which the industrial squabbles inside and outside the industry had drawn sales down, all the popular Fleet Street papers were lined up like racehorses at the starting gate, ready for a spring circulation drive. It was no time to be miserly. Joy was still asking for £50,000.

'Actually, I would have given her as much as the budget could stand,' Jameson said afterwards. 'But we settled for £40,000.'

151

The question then was who was actually to write the series on which the *Express* was ready to spend so much money. Jameson and Tory had agreed with Joy's that, apart from the story of the Great Escape, the series would be, in essence, *The Greatest Love Story Ever Told*. The words would be Joy's, or at least she would have final approval of what was to be published. It was Tory to whom Joy had turned and who had negotiated the deal with her. That, he believed, entitled him to stake a claim.

The problem for Jameson was that although Tory was to go on to become an enormously popular columnist he had, at that time, little experience of producing a lengthy narrative. On the other hand, the features department of the *Express* contained a wealth of talent for just that kind of project, writers who were expert at persuading a bought-up name to tell rather more than he or she had intended and polishing up the result for maximum reader appeal.

'But it was Tory's story,' Jameson decided. 'He deserved his revenge. But I made sure he would have some back-up.'

Joy and Tory set up an elaborately clandestine rendezvous. Joy chose the spot: the Airport Hilton in Atlanta, Georgia. 'You check in,' she instructed in the last of their conspiratorial calls. 'We'll come there after dark. We'll be in disguise.'

So it proved. Tory arrived at the rather shabby motel-style Hilton after a harrowing journey in which he had been afraid to take his eyes off the little suitcase he carried that contained $75,000 in the small bills that such a transaction seemed to call for. At dusk came a knock at the door of his room. He opened it to a ludicrous apparition, Joy and Keith in blackface... 'Imagine the worst kind of Ali Baba make-up, real pantomime slap. They looked like a couple of escaped circus clowns.'

Ever the gentleman, Tory invited the pair in. They headed for his bathroom where they spent an hour splashing about to remove the black greasepaint. 'The bath, the walls, the towels everything was covered with the stuff,' Tory recalled. 'God knows what the hotel thought.'

Restored to her glowing blonde self, Joy was ready to receive her due. She allowed herself a moment of gloating over the packets of crisp dollar bills then snapped the suitcase shut. The *Express* men never saw it again.

The first of Tory's reinforcements arrived the following day, Bill Lovelace, the paper's chief photographer and a veteran of many such exploits. Taciturn and ingenious, he was a reassuring presence both for the nervous Tory and the highly excitable Joy.

Joy decided a new disguise was called for. Something not so exotic that it would attract attention – and not something that would rub off on everyone. 'I know', she cried. 'Nuns! Keith, too.'

That was fine by Tory and Lovelace. Great pictures. But Atlanta was not exactly abrim with theatrical – or ecclesiastical – costumers. It took half a day to get the outfits together; the other half was devoted to photographing Joy and Keith looking improbably demure in their habits and wimples. Lovelace airfreighted the film to London and, fearful that they might attract attention, the little circus hit the road.

By that time they were five. Jameson had despatched Brian Vine from the *Express*'s New York bureau, to play the heavy. He, too, was out for revenge. He knew he had been outclassed by Jill Evans back in Orem and he wanted to even the score. Rubicund, belligerent and loud, Vine was hardly a discreet presence. But he was an accomplished manipulator and just the man to help Tory throw together the kind of story the *Express* wanted to run in Joy's name.

'For about a week we never spent two nights in the same place,' Tory remembered. 'Joy was terrified that the FBI was on her trail. Vine and I were more concerned that the competition would somehow track us down.'

The *Mirror* did not need to go after them. Through advertising agency contacts in London it had already discovered that the *Express* was booking television slots and a series of high-powered spots was already in production. There could be little doubt of what was in the offing.

Molloy allowed himself a quiet chuckle. The bait had been swallowed. Sorry as he might be not to be turning his guns on the *Sun*, he was just as ready to do the *Express* a bad turn.

Jameson was a friend, as well as his former deputy. He hoped it wouldn't hurt too much.

In the *Mirror* office the mood changed. Shillum made discreet preparations. Beam and Wigmore took Austin and the others into custody. Buckland collected Steve from Los Angeles and took him to Mexico, safe from the revenge of Joy – and the *Mirror's* competitors.

Crammed into a rented car, the *Express* team and their prizes covered long stretches of highway, overnighting in a succession of grisly motels, eating in greasy spoons. If anyone had been looking for them they would not have been hard to trace: a nun who dug out a jar of goop from under her robes and spattered it over everything she ate; a red-faced Englishman who was habitually rude to the help.

Along the way Tory and Vine debriefed Joy, shaped and polished the story of her life before and after Kirk, and in a series of furtive telephone calls from out-of-the way locations, filed the result to London. Jameson himself put the copy together with Lovelace's artful pictures to make a high-impact front page and several more inside: Joy stuffing the brassiere that Keith wore under his nun's habit; Joy, stubby as ever in her swimming costume, playing the bathing beauty on a deserted beach.

The series was to run for a full week. The story was essentially the one Joy had been offering all along. It was fragrant with innocence and injured maidenly pride. The Mormons had been beastly. So had the British. It would have been impossible for her and Keith to get a fair trial because no one in Britain could understand what she had felt for Kirk.

She had planned to escape from the very beginning, Joy said. She had only stayed around for so long 'to play cat-and-mouse with the Epsom police'. Oh, well. If that's what she said...

In one episode though, Joy did display a belated stirring of conscience for the people who had been most harmed by her compulsive self-promotion – her parents. While she had been teasing the Epsom coppers and trying to make herself a star, Joy's mother and father had beggared themselves to support her.

154

The strain of dealing with his daughter's predicament forced her father, an ill man in any case, to resign from his school post.

'He sacrificed everything for me,' Joy told Tory and Vine with melodramatic remorse. 'He earned only £300 a month. On two occasions I know he sent me his whole cheque, because it was the exact amount in dollars that I knew he was paid.' Trust Joy to know the precise figure on her father's salary cheque.

The *Express* had no sooner begun to crank up the pre-publication publicity for its great triumph when there was a bizarre challenge to its exclusive right to Joy's story. Bob Guccione, the publisher of *Penthouse*, a glossy flesh magazine, applied for an injunction to prevent the series being published. He claimed that he, in person, had signed an agreement with Joy in the early hours of the morning that she had fled Britain. According to the story told in court, where the *Express* rushed to contest, the injunction, Guccione had met Joy and Keith after Tory had taken her home from the premiere.

The prospect of the *Express* being gagged by this totally unexpected development gave the *Mirror* a bad twenty-four hours as well but a judge declined to continue the injunction. If Mr Guccione had a case, he said, he must take it up after the material had been published. The *Express* pulled out all stops on the great organ of publicity. Joy and Keith simpered from billboards and TV screens all over Britain.

The day before the *Express* was to launch its epic series, the McKinney contingent was installed in a series of rooms on the eighth floor of a shabby seaside hotel in Myrtle Beach, South Carolina, where the arrival of a pair of nuns travelling with an escort of three shifty-looking men attracted no special attention. At first. No decision had been made about whether Joy's whereabouts should be disclosed or whether the *Express* should admit she was in their care. She was, after all, a fugitive from justice, at least in Britain.

Even though she insisted on keeping her disguise, Joy had finally ceased to worry about all of that. She was delirious with excitement. In just a few hours the world would be able to read her story – the version of it anyway that she and her companions had devised. At last, people would be able to read *The Greatest Love Story Ever Told*. At last people would know what she had suffered. At last she would be famous not just for some silly old police mess-up but because she was a Great Lover.

Molloy came to his decision. He was ready to take the risk. He told Tony Miles he believed that once the *Express* had fired off its costly broadside it was highly unlikely that the DPP would prosecute the *Mirror*. Or him. He was going to blast back at the *Express*, blow the enemy out of the water. Miles was a cautious man but a tabloid journalist to the core. 'It's your decision,' he said. 'If they send you to prison, I'll come with you.'

His nerves taut as the miles of paper spanning the huge presses in the basement of the building, Molloy, unlocked his safe and handed over the layouts he had prepared to the astonished production staff. 'Only one headline on Page One,' he instructed: 'The Real McKinney.'

'Joy to The World...' they sang, opening the champagne.

Joy was first to hear of the catastrophe. Impatient for early plaudits, she telephoned Annette Thatcher. The bad news had already reached North London: the *Mirror* was on the streets with the whole story of Joy's life in Los Angeles and the bondage pictures.

It was the tabloid scoop of the decade. The first bootleg pages of the *Mirror* to reach the *Express* – every newspaper has informers in rival offices – caused pandemonium. The presses down below were still spilling out the anodyne version of Joy's story that Vine and Tory had concocted; Lovelace's pictures of her and Keith in their nuns' habits peeked coyly from the front page. A couple of hundred yards to the west vans were pulling away from the *Mirror* with bundles of papers that displayed Joy in all her naked splendour. Little doubt which would do better on the news-stands.

The *Express* newsdesk, stunned into helplessness, was trying to reach the minders but they were all gathered in Joy's room, where she was listening to Annette. Just as well.

'Joy's reaction was astounding,' Tory recalled. 'She threw down the phone and rushed for the windows, clawing her way up the curtains. She was dressed in her nun's habit. She looked like a giant bat.'

Clinging to the curtains, Joy swung out on to the balcony of the hotel room and started to clamber over the guardrail. Tory grabbed her ankles and hauled her back. He and Lovelace wrapped the curtains around her as a restraint. Vine retrieved the phone and got through to London. There was no time to wring their hands over being so grandly scooped, however. Joy was squealing and squirming, trying to shed her voluminous costume. What on earth were they to do with her? Keith, familiar perhaps with such mega-tantrums, merely looked on.

The journalists, however, had never seen a performance like it. Seriously worried, they decided to get Joy to a hospital. Tory was full of praise for Vine. 'Brian was superb. He gave the emergency ward some cock-and-bull story about a nervous breakdown and explained that the poor woman had to be got back home to her convent. They took her into a room for a little while and she came out in a wheelchair. She was like a zombie.'

Vine telephoned Joy's parents. Like Keith, the McKinney's seemed only mildly surprised at Joy's state. They were about five hours drive away, they said. They would be there as soon as they could. The *Express* men prayed that Joy's sedation would hold out.

By the time the McKinneys arrived it was early morning. The moment Joy saw her father, Tory remembered, she lunged at him, seizing his forearm between her teeth and worrying it like a dog. Blood flowed. Whatever the hospital had given her was wearing off and she broke away, running down the hotel corridor screaming. Inevitably, someone called the police. A pair of state troopers shouldered their way into the roomful of exhausted and distracted people.

'Huge men,' Tory remembered. 'Big hats. Dark glasses – even indoors.' Vine, bombastic as ever, tried to explain what was going on, taking the cops back to the beginning: the kidnap, the Mormons, the bail-jumping. As he burbled on the shades came off, the cops' eyes widened. 'Eventually they gave us a few words of advice,' said Tory. 'Get her over the state line.'

Jameson took it like a man. He strode out of the gloom-ridden *Express* building and headed for the *Mirror*'s favourite pub, the White Hart, in Fetter Lane, universally known – most appropriately at that moment – as the Stab In The Back. Instinct told him what would be going on there and, sure enough, he walked into a scene of riotous self-congratulation. 'Only a handful of people in the bar had played any part in getting the story,' Molloy recalled. 'But the entire staff wanted to celebrate the great victory.' Jameson waited for the cheers that greeted him to subside and thrust both hands in the air. 'I surrender!'

'What else could I do?' he asked afterwards. 'That was the way things were in Fleet Street. Despite everything, they were all my mates. They'd done a marvelous job, much as it hurt me to say so. What could I do but buy them all a drink?'

Aftermath

As I said up front, this book is a period piece. It was written as much to celebrate an epochal Fleet Street caper as to cash in on Joyce McKinney's notoriety. Despite the running repairs and revisions, the story is located firmly in 1970s Britain and the values that prevailed then.

Joy was never going to fade gracefully out of the public gaze. Certainly not out of Kirk Anderson's. Intermittently, she returned to Utah to stalk Kirk, who married not long after the abrupt ending of his mission. It was after one of those visits that Joy first made the claim that she had been attacked – in one version by Mormons, in another by a Mormon dog.

In 1984 she was arrested outside Salt Lake City airport, where Kirk worked. In her car was a length of rope and handcuffs and a notebook recording Kirk's movements. Joy was charged with harassment and lying to police. She did not appear for the trial and the case was dismissed.

Intermittent run-ins with the law in America began before 1979 when Joy realised that the FBI was closing in on the mobile home where she and Keith were shacked up. She tried to make a deal with *Men Only*, a girlie magazine run by British strip-club magnate Paul Raymond. She offered to pose nude for £2,000 but she wanted the spread to include photographs of her being arrested. Raymond passed.

When she was hauled into court a judge said he would give her bail only if she checked into a psychiatric clinic. 'I'm not going to be locked up with a bunch of loonies!' she snapped. Her court-appointed lawyer hissed: 'Say yes, say yes!'

Eventually the pair pleaded guilty to falsifying passport applications and received brief suspended sentences. By then, in Britain, the Attorney General had told the House of Commons that there was to be no extradition application.

Keith went home to California, where he was last heard of selling plumbing supplies. Joy became involved in the Right to Life movement, her unmistakable image occasionally popping up in news pictures of demonstrations outside abortion clinics.

After that it was Animal Rights. She established a small menagerie in a house near the Kentucky border left to her by her grandmother, that included the pitbull Hamburger – apparently the 'Booger' that was cloned in Korea.

Booger was soon in trouble and Joy with him. The dog was reported to have attacked a jogger and was taken into custody by the local sheriff. Joy, it seems, broke into to the pound where Booger was being held and sprung him. 'I love pitbulls,' she explained when she was charged with causing damage. 'They're such sympathetic animals.'

More bizarre developments followed in 2004, when one of several ponies she owned somehow lost part of a hind leg. In a complicated plan to get money to buy the poor beast an artificial limb, Joy was said to have persuaded a 15-year-old boy to break into a house in Tennessee. She was charged with criminal conspiracy to commit aggravated burglary and contributing to the delinquency of a minor – a strange echo of the suggestions about Joy's influence on younger people heard back in Orem years earlier. In familiar fashion, she jumped bail and bolted across the state line.

Periodically, British journalists would turn up at Joy's door. They were treated to a familiar refrain: 'I loved Kirk and all I really wanted was to see his blond-haired babies running round my home', she told Ian Cobain in 1999. 'Nobody can understand what it is to lose the man you love to a cult, and I believe that is what the Mormons are. Back in Britain then nobody knew what a cult was.'

She was far more upbeat when she arrived in Seoul, nearly a decade later, as Bernann McKinney.

Five puppies had been cloned from a scrap of Booger's ear which she had preserved.

The company that carried out the procedure told Associated Press it would normally have charged £50,000 but, in exchange for the promotional help the lady had promised, they did it for half price.

Presented to the Korean media, 'Bernann' told a dramatic story to explain why it was so important to her that Booger should be replicated. He had saved her life years earlier when she had been attacked by 'an enraged bull mastiff'. This sounded like a highly coloured version of an event she had often referred to but on that occasion she did not claim it was a Mormon mastiff.

Booger, she related, had driven off the attacking dog but not before it had shredded her left arm to the elbow, torn open one of her legs and ripped three fingers from her left hand. All this damage had been repaired by skilful surgeons. Throughout her convalescence, faithful Booger remained at her side, giving her the will to go on.

It did appear that Bernann had been injured at some time. There was a prominent scar on her arm and she walked with a limp. She sometimes used a wheelchair, although she had no difficulty moving around for the cameras without it.

Bernann told reporters she was a grandmother. She had sold her home to pay for the cloning. Before the accident she had been a university drama teacher in Los Angeles. Now she planned to write a Hollywood script about the cloning.

In the furore that followed the television broadcasts of her with the squirming puppies, Bernann at first denied that she was actually Joyce. In Avery County, however, where she had not been seen for a couple of years, she was recognised immediately. From the office where a fat file of summonses and writs awaited Joy's reappearance, courthouse clerk Julia Henson said drily: 'She is a person of note in our little community.' The lawyer Joy had hired to defend her on the Tennessee charges, David Crockett (sic), said: 'It's rather brave of her to show herself like that. She's still a wanted fugitive in this state. But she is a rather bizarre character.'

The identity Joy adopted for the Korean adventure was hardly up to her previous standards: Bernann was merely her middle name. The passport details and social security number that were on record belonged to Joy. The Los Angeles address on the cards

161

she handed out did not exist. Soon afterwards, she disappeared from Seoul, leaving behind the five puppies – and a promise to pay the bill for £25,000.

All that, together with the accounts of Joy's behaviour after the *Express* fiasco, that were not available for the first version of the book, raises the question of whether she might be less an amusing eccentric than someone who ought to be locked up with a bunch of loonies, to use her own term. I can only say that it did not seem like that at the time – and not just to voracious journalists.

Following up the cloning story, *The Times* tracked down the barrister who had been briefed to defend Keith May, Bob Marshall-Andrews, now a Labour MP. He had been looking forward to the Old Bailey trial and still regretted that it had never taken place. Joyce McKinney, he recalled, had been 'a woman of considerable presence'.

Also by Anthony Delano:

SLIP-UP:

How Fleet Street found Ronnie Biggs
and Scotland Yard Lost Him

The story behind the scoop

By Anthony Delano

ISBN: 978-0-9558238-3-1

Perhaps the best analysis of Fleet Street at work ever written.
– *Keith Waterhouse*

No journalist can afford to miss this cautionary tale… the story of the
in-fighting and downfall of all concerned has one rolling in the aisles.
Mr Delano's eye is astute, his ear a credit to his profession at any
level; and his wit is accompanied by the ability to write clear English.
– *The Times*

Marvellously funny and told with ease and wit... The best stories are
sometimes the ones behind the news. There never was a more hilarious
tale. – *Daily Mirror*

Anthony Delano, a reporter of much experience, has written the most
useful, intellectually coherent and – yes – serious action-study of the
British Press that anyone has given us for years... and hysterically
funny… A beautifully articulated case-study of the Code of the Street
in action. – *Bruce Page, New Statesman*

The funniest book of the summer. With expertly witty hands, Delano
uproariously describes how 'the biggest comeback of a condemned
man since the Resurrection' was bungled... Lovely fun.
– *Cosmopolitan*

Delano mercilessly exposes the savage Fleet Street competition that
underlay the Biggs scoop, and the tale is pacey, absorbing, humorous.
– *New Society*

Has an authentic ring. For anyone interested in the inner workings of a popular newspaper, it is enlightening and amusing. A readable and entertaining piece of work. – *Listener*

I'd say it's the funniest book about Fleet Street since Evelyn Waugh's *Scoop*. I stayed up half the night to finish it. It's one of those you-can't-put-it-down books. SLIP-UP includes some devastating portraits of Fleet Street characters. Delano's wicked pen spares no one. – *Phillip Knightley,* **Press Gazette**

A Billy Wilder-style comedy of muddle, mistrust, and misplaced zeal. – *New York Times*

Gripping… Delano tells it superbly. It's hard to think of a book since *Scoop* in which double dealing, grappling ambition, spectacular successes and the glaring ineptitudes of daily journalism are examined so sharply and with such wit. – *The Australian*

A story worth telling, not only for entertainment, but also for the light it throws on journalistic practices. The characters are vividly and sympathetically presented. – *Times Literary Supplement*

Dead-eye Delano has done it... He has taken on two of those worthy – if somewhat frowsty – British institutions, Scotland Yard and the *Daily Express* and demolished them with wit, pace and a keen eye... A hilarious straight-through read. Very, very good value for those who like a laugh. For journalists it is a must. – *The Scotsman*

Revel Barker Publishing

Other titles in this collection of classic books about newspapers and journalism

Crying All The Way To The Bank
(Liberace v. the Daily Mirror and Cassandra)
By Revel Barker
Foreword by Vera Baird QC
ISBN: 978-0-9558238-7-9

It's the Liberace Show…! – *Time* magazine

Bizarre and hilarious… Nothing shorter than a paperback could achieve a balanced report of the brilliance of the advocacy and summing-up. – *Hugh Cudlipp*

Cross-examinations and a brilliant closing speech had me barking with laughter – *Law Society Gazette*

Cassandra
At His Finest And Funniest
By William Neil Connor
ISBN: 978-0-9558238-2-4

Millions of his followers throughout the English-speaking world will treasure this book of some of his finest and funniest writing. – *Hugh Cudlipp*

Ladies of The Street
By Liz Hodgkinson
ISBN: 978-0-9558238-5-5

An entertaining historical overview, charting the gradual rise of women into positions of power and influence. This book finally gives Fleet Street's pioneering women their due. – *Roy Greenslade*

The Best Of Vincent Mulchrone
A lifetime of wit and observation of the folly and splendour of his fellow humans by the Daily Mail's finest reporter.
ISBN: 978-0-9558238-1-7

He could penetrate in a flash to the heart of a story in a few deceptively simple words. – *Vere Harmsworth*

A Crooked Sixpence

By Murray Sayle

ISBN: 978-0-9558238-4-8

The best novel about journalism – ever. – *Phillip Knightley*

Wonderful – the best book about British popular journalism – *Roy Greenslade*

The best novel never published. – *Anthony Delano.*

A classic – *Peter Stothard*, Times Literary Supplement

Forgive Us Our Press Passes

By Ian Skidmore

Revised and expanded, 2008
ISBN: 978-0-9558238-0-0

…should be made required reading for every child-in-a-suit populating what passes for our newsrooms these days. – *Press Gazette*

Hilarious –*Start The Week* (BBC Radio 4)

The Upper Pleasure Garden

By Gordon M Williams

ISBN: 978-0-9558238-6-2

The flavour of this sort of journalistic life is caught as well as in any novel I can remember. – *Sunday Times*

A most entertaining and intelligent novel. – *Evening Standard*

Everything throbs with life, vibrates with individuality... for sheer *elan vital* it's the next best thing to surf-bathing. – *Irish Times*

More details: *www.booksaboutjournalism.com*

 Revel Barker Publishing

265290BV00003B/54/P

9 780955 823886